Somewhere in France

Somewhere in France
A Tommy's Guide to Life on the Western Front

William & Geoffrey Whittaker

AMBERLEY

First published 2014

Amberley Publishing
The Hill, Stroud
Gloucestershire, GL5 4EP

www.amberley-books.com

British Library Cataloguing in Publication Data.
A catalogue record for this book is available from the British Library.

ISBN 978 1 4456 3671 9 (paperback)
ISBN 978 1 4456 3689 4 (ebook)

Typeset in 10pt on 12pt Sabon.
Typesetting and Origination by Amberley Publishing.
Printed in the UK.

Contents

Introduction

Attitudes to military service and war were very different in the Britain of 1914 to those a century later. The British Empire, proudly shown in red on the maps in primary schoolrooms throughout the country, was the cornerstone of every child's first geography lesson. The story of the great battles and the heroes who led them – Nelson of Trafalgar, Wellington of Waterloo, Marlborough of Blenheim, Wolfe of Quebec, Clive of India – were at the heart of history lessons. The recent scramble for new colonies in Africa had left Britain with even more red on the map and in control of much of the best economic potential of that vast continent.

The messages that we never lost wars, that we had a right to rule and that the introduction of our trade, our religion and our forms of government were good for all the subjects of the king were taken for granted.

Jingoism or chauvinistic patriotism summed up the attitude to war. In the words of the popular ditty which was sung in clubs and music halls everywhere:

> We don't want to fight
> But by Jingo if we do

We've got the ships.

We've got the men

And we've got the money too.

The latest evidence of military triumph was as recent as the crushing of the Boers in the South African wars and the establishment of the richest state in Africa only ten years before the First World War began.

Then there was the whole question of Honour. This British trait was firmly rooted in society. Honour derived from courtly etiquette as old as tales of King Arthur and the Knights of the Round Table. It was deeply embodied in the class system and emphasised in the norms of behaviour instilled into the upper classes at their public schools and the rules of the games invented in Britain and exported to the world. The phrase 'It isn't cricket' is still in use today to indicate how things should be done by honourable people.

In 1914, Britain's right to rule the world was coming under threat. Germany under Kaiser Wilhelm II was bent on equalising armed strength with Britain, and especially challenging its traditional naval supremacy. Commercial rivalries were growing and the share in world trade was shifting slowly away from Britain.

All these factors meant that every young man was expected to don military uniform, if necessary, to meet any perceived threat to national supremacy and to uphold the honour of the nation. It was deemed noble to lay down one's life for this cause and to teach a lesson to any foreigner who threatened the status quo.

Historians still differ about the causes of the First World War, but the immediate trigger for British intervention was Germany's invasion of 'little' Belgium and the need to 'honour' the alliance with France. The national mood was overwhelmingly in favour of going to war and when volunteers were called for in 1915, to boost the regular forces that went to the front at the outbreak, men flocked to the recruiting stations in vast numbers.

Such was the national psyche that not to volunteer was seen to be an act of cowardice and those who did not come forward were increasingly ostracised.

Importantly, the rigid class system meant that virtually all the officers were drawn from the upper classes and instilled with the public school ethos, while the lower classes, however intelligent and well educated, knew their place and were consigned to the 'other ranks'.

This social order was accepted without challenge and the private soldier was ready to take orders from those destined to rule him and to put up with all sorts of privations, notably living conditions, which were often miserable.

This goes a long way towards explaining why death and destruction on a colossal scale was tolerated. Of course, religious belief was still widespread and the war meant that God's will was being worked out.

How different are attitudes today, when the death of a single soldier can bring the whole justification for military intervention into question!

This book seeks to show just what it was like for the young men who volunteered, and the conscripts who later followed them, to serve at the front line in Flanders and north-eastern France during the First World War. The story is told through extracts from the 270 letters written by my father, William Whittaker, to his parents, Thomas and Isabella Whittaker, who lived in Burnley, Lancashire, during his four years of service with the British Army.

He was eighteen years old when he volunteered, below the legal age of nineteen, giving as his birth date 22 January 1896, though he was actually born on that date in 1897. The authorities turned a blind eye to what was common practice among young men eager to serve.

William, known as Willie to his parents, joined up in June 1915, and the early letters were from Chelsea Barracks, London, where he did his initial training and then Hampshire, where he did field training with the Royal Army Medical Corps, which he had requested to join.

In the autumn of 1915 he was posted to Flanders. After some time in Belgium he was moved to north-eastern France where he served for most of the war at the front as part of 41st Sanitary Section.

The letters were acquired by my elder brother on the death of our father at the age of eighty-six in 1983. They were all in original condition and mostly in their official green envelopes. I had no idea of their existence until they were given to me shortly before my brother himself died. Unfortunately none of the letters to Willie from home have survived. There must have been more than 270 letters from home but there was no way a soldier moving regularly from place to place under war conditions could retain any but non-essential items.

Willie was a highly intelligent man and wrote in a fluent literary style. His descriptions of the war itself and the way of life of the troops are so compelling and vivid that I determined to put extracts together in the form of this book as a permanent record. This also gave me the opportunity to describe incidents and add anecdotes which were not spelled out in the letters but which he had recounted to me as a youngster. Many of these he had not been able to put in his letters home because of the censorship rules which prohibited any material which might be thought to damage morale in Britain. It was not permitted even to mention where the troops were, so almost all the letters are simply headed 'Somewhere in France', which presented itself as an appropriate title for this narrative.

I have added some personal details about his life to add colour to the narrative and include some material about his early life and later career as a bank manager in a Northern industrial town. Interestingly, I was also able to recount his contribution to the Second World War where he was appointed commanding officer of the local Home Guard with the rank of Major. He truly was a 'Captain Mainwaring' of *Dad's Army* fame both in his civilian and Army posts!

The letters provide a fascinating insight to the subtle social changes, accelerated by the war, which were to lead quite rapidly to very different attitudes economically and politically, as well as the emancipation of women and the beginnings of the erosion of the class system. It was a different world that awaited the troops on demobilisation.

Geoffrey Whittaker
2014

1

Britons Your Country Needs You

For a century now historians have analysed the origins of the 1914–18 war. Hundreds of books have investigated the complex political situation, the web of diplomacy which linked Germany with Austria-Hungary, England with France and the labyrinthine network of Balkan alliances involving Russia, Serbia and Bulgaria.

The determination of Franz-Joseph II, the man who was destined to be the last Hapsburg emperor, urged on by his hawkish foreign minister Matscheko, to subdue the Serbs and absorb them into the Austro-Hungarian Empire was the trigger for the assassination of the Crown Prince Ferdinand in Sarajevo. This in turn led to the declaration of war by Franz-Joseph on Serbia, in retaliation for the death of his son, which brought Russia in on the side of the Serbs. This activated the alliance between Russia and Serbia and left the weak Hapsburg Army fighting hopelessly on two fronts, which in turn brought in Germany on the side of its ally Austria, thus giving the German people and many historians the conviction that it was not Germany who had started the war.

Hindsight has led to the above objective assessment of the events which led to the invasion of Belgium by Germany in

1914. In Britain however there was no doubt at the time that this pre-emptive move started the 'world' conflict, and it certainly drew in the British Expeditionary Force to Flanders and north-eastern France to meet the threat to their French allies. It was clear that Germany was bent on expansion, and the build-up of its navy was seen as a threat to Britannia's right to rule the waves – Germany's aggression had to be met by force.

The first soldiers of the BEF were all regulars, but as the potential threat posed by Germany was realised, and probably exaggerated accounts of atrocities committed against Belgian civilians were circulated, popular sentiment called upon able-bodied young men to volunteer to join the Army, which they did, cheerfully, in countless numbers. Posters featuring the head and torso of General Lord Kitchener, the legendary hero of Khartoum, appeared on every hoarding, his finger pointing at the viewer seemingly from all angles, with the caption 'Britons I need you, join your country's army! God save the King.' Kitchener himself was to be an early casualty of the war, drowning when the Royal Navy cruiser he was sailing in sank with all hands in 1915.

It was against this background that William Whittaker became one of those young men who answered the call and volunteered.

Willie, as he was known to his parents, was the son of Thomas and Isabella Whittaker of Burnley in Lancashire. He was born on 22 January 1897. Thomas's mother had died in his birth and, as his widowed father already had two infant children to look after, Thomas was brought up in the lower middle-class home of his grandparents. Isabella, *née* Varley, was from a working-class background. They married young and Willie, who was their only child, was born a year later, when they were still only twenty-one years old. His father (Tom) managed a tobacconist shop in Burnley and his mother (Bella) was a winder in a local cotton mill. Both were educated, however. Tom was well schooled, a voracious reader and something of a philosopher and lateral thinker – traits passed on to his son – while Bella, although starting work at the age of twelve, had been in part-time education for some years – half a day at the mill and half a day at school.

Willie had a normal, happy childhood and although there were elements of the street urchin in some of his activities, such as hunting down alley cats, a pastime known as 'fusker hunting', he was well brought up to conventional Victorian standards, with a high moral code. He was a regular attendee at the chapel Sunday school, learned to swim in Burnley's North Street baths, where he was in the water polo team, and, very importantly, learned to play the violin at the instigation of his musical uncle Jim. Willie, who was an intelligent boy, qualified for Burnley Grammar School, where he made lifelong friends in John Kippax and Harry Preston, both of whom were mentioned regularly in his letters home. As was normal at the time for all but the wealthy and highly academic, he left school at the age of fourteen and went to work as a debt collector for another uncle, John Whittaker, but soon moved to a junior position on the local newspaper – the *Burnley Express* – before getting what he fully expected to be a career job as a clerk in the Burnley County Court, where he was employed at the outbreak of war.

Although he was only eighteen years old (the official age for volunteers was nineteen), Willie volunteered for the Royal Army Medical Corps, the RAMC, early in 1915. He lied about his age, giving his birth year as 1896. The authorities were no doubt pleased to have intelligent boys who could be trained for more complex tasks than would be required from those joining the infantry and accepted him into the Sanitary Corps of the RAMC, turning a blind eye to the age question, as they no doubt did in thousands of other cases. Willie was called up a few weeks later, reporting to Chelsea Barracks in London, after a long and tiring journey on 3 June 1915.

His first letter, just a few lines written that very evening, is quoted in full:

Dear Parents,

Arrived all safe and sound. Travelled a long way on the tube, rode on moving staircases, descended in lifts and experienced many new things. We have seen our beds for tonight and they are quite alright. We have not been sworn in nor medically tested yet but have signed the forms.

I write this just after tea, bread, jam and good butter, and tonight at 7 o'clock we had a free concert by artists from several theatres. Except for the journey the day has been uneventful and I will let you have fuller particulars later.

Willie.
P.S. Best lot of fellows I ever saw. [3/6/15]

The postscript to this letter is revealing. The volunteers were fine young men, well motivated and cheerful. They were confident that what they were doing was right and honourable.

They were also optimistic, for after all, most of them thought it would be all over by Christmas!

It emerged much later in the letters that his parents had influenced the decision to join the RAMC. No doubt they saw it as an interesting opportunity to further Willie's skills but also perhaps shrewdly thinking that it might be a safer option than for their son to be in the firing line. Willie was to pen a mild rebuke to his parents, after seeing infantrymen marching back from a battle, to the effect that he was perhaps not doing his bit. In fact, the sanitary service was to save thousands of lives, whereas the only agenda for the infantryman was to kill or be killed.

Willie's companions from Burnley on 3 June were a friend from North Street Chapel Sunday School, Percy Shoesmith, and an older man, Billy Worswick. Percy was only seventeen and had added two years on to his age. The three Burnley lads were inseparable for a few weeks, but Percy seems to have been rather puny and moreover there were worries about his heart as he had collapsed one day on parade. An hour-long examination at one of the medicals, which all recruits went through after joining up, led to his parents being contacted. They wrote to confirm his true age and Percy was sent home to join the reserve until he was at least nineteen. Billy Worswick received bad news that his eight-year-old son had been injured by a motorbike and was sent home. He returned later so presumably all was well, but the delay in his training meant that he was behind the original unit and so did not form part of the same section when they were posted to France.

The new recruits to the Sanitary Corps were billeted in a Wesleyan chapel adjacent to Chelsea Barracks and were kept together as specialists rather than mixing with infantry volunteers. They were kitted out and were told that they would spend about three months of basic training in England followed by a posting abroad:

We shall be rigged out tomorrow in our khaki and you would be surprised what stuff we had to buy viz: button stick, soap, soap box, metal polish, brush, two dusters. Clasp for kit bag etc. [6/6/15]

It seems rather unfair when compared to values a century later that recruits had to purchase items essential to keeping their kit in order out of their meagre pay – a pittance of a few shillings a week.

The emphasis in training was on hard physical work, mostly in the form of route marches to make the men fit, some lectures and trade training in various sanitary procedures. There was the unpleasant experience of inoculation, which was in a rudimentary stage of development, and then transfer to a country camp – Blackdown in Hampshire – for more general military training and war games.

Willie revelled in the outdoor work and was bursting with health. His favourite phrase was that he was 'in the pink'. The long marches also gave him a good idea of Greater London, for which he had a growing attachment:

We have had a fine march to Hampstead Heath. It is glorious there: I think it will be the highest point for miles around London and the fine breeze there was so refreshing after a hot march. [6/7/15]

We had a lovely route march through Hyde Park, Kensington Gardens and Regents Park. We left the billet at 9 o'clock and had a ten minute halt in Hyde Park and then marched to Regents Park, where we arrived at 11 o'clock. A free rest of an hour was given us there and, falling in, we marched back to billet arriving for dinner at 1 o'clock. Mornings like this, as you can understand, are very enjoyable. [6/6/15]

We have had a twenty mile route march today and my feet have never felt better. We paraded at 8.30 this morning and then set off carrying mess tin, knapsack and water bottle to Richmond Park. The officers were on horseback and did not forget to give us one or two short halts on the way. On arriving at the park (which is a natural one and is of enormous size and pastorally pretty) we had a rest of half an hour during which time tents were pitched and flags raised by a few fellows who had preceded us on motor lorries. About 12 o'clock we commenced physical drill and sprinting, which carried on until about 12.15 and then had a lecture on military etiquette. We then had a substantial dinner and rested for about an hour. For drink we had water drawn from a nearby running ditch, sterilised and purified by men of the corps. We returned, had tea, a swimming bath parade and were dismissed, finishing a day which to me has been the most enjoyable since I came down. I just feel like knocking a bull down. [15/6/15]

We had a great route march today. We went by Wimbledon Common and several small, pretty villages to Robin Hood's Gate then through the park, which is profusely wooded and in the clearings of which are large herds of wild deer, to Richmond. It is a beautiful village, all the habitations being villas or ivy covered cottages. The view, looking down to the winding Thames, is glorious. Days like this make one feel one is on holiday and although these do not occur every day one quickly forgets the unpleasant ones. In my little straw bed I sleep as sound as I have ever done in my life. [29/6/15]

The emphasis on physical fitness as an essential part of the preparation of all the troops shows just how thorough the training was. Willie was clearly bursting with health and evidence of his superb condition was emphatically demonstrated by the following incident:

Would you believe it but today your Willie, the thin one, was used as an example to show how to do physical drill – some boy! I shouldn't have written this if I thought many were going to read it but you will understand I felt a little proud. [15/8/15]

Surprisingly, in the light of later practice, medicals do not seem to have been required before enlistment or surely Percy Shoesmith would have been found out, but once in training the medicals seem to have been quite thorough. The recruits had an amusing encounter with the M.O.:

The doctor who passed us was a real sport and some of his chaff was really good. We went to him stripped to the waist, seven of us. Worswick went up and he said 'Ah corporal, you must feed this man up'. Another fellow who had a long scar on his leg because of a varicose vein operation was asked if the vein hurt him. On hearing the reply 'no' the doctor said 'Ah well, I suppose you had it done for ornamentation'. He told me to carry my head and shoulders better and I should be alright. [4/6/15]

The worst experience was inoculation, which consisted of three treatments with cow pox that left large scars on the upper arm that were visible for life:

Today we have been inoculated and the experience, though not painful, was unnerving. One has to bare his arm to the shoulder, the nurse paints it with iodine and the doctor then inserts the needle syringe, which is pushed under the skin by about an inch and a half to inject a certain amount of vaccine from typhoid germs. Four of our strongest and biggest chaps fainted today after inoculation but I am glad to say that none of our three have felt any bad effects except the stiffening of the arm which is quite usual. [10/6/15]

In spite of there being no initial reaction, poor Percy suffered badly:

The vaccination is a most rotten thing, Percy having been in bed for seven days because of it. I have been given leave today with instructions to 'take it easy' and I feel like it. About seven of us have had our arms examined and been told they are going on quite well, although to us the mattery scabs are ugly things to look at. The arm is nicely cleaned and dressed every two or three days. We are having a concert tomorrow night and I was booked for a violin solo but I shall have to cry off because of my arm. [27/7/15]

This was the first mention of Willie's skill as a violinist, which was to be an important feature of his life in France during the next four years.

The training in specialist sanitary skills took the form of lectures and practical work:

Yesterday we commenced a series of six lectures under one of the Lieutenants on water supply and I think it will be very interesting. [17/6/15]

Up to the present I have learned how to test water and how to sterilise and clarify it, how to make latrines, urine pits and grease traps. [10/6/15]

There were other optional classes; the one described here, in the French language, was obviously set up in the knowledge that most of the men would soon be in France. Willie's performance was a tribute to the tuition he had received at Burnley Grammar School. One must wonder, however, if the promise of home-made cake had something to do with the good attendance:

Last night the three of us and many more attended a free French class for soldiers. It is conducted by London ladies

*who give their services and text books free. We are split
into classes of six or eight pupils. The teacher straightaway
commended me for my excellent pronunciation and asked if
I had learned it from a Frenchman. We have to attend these
classes on Mondays, Wednesdays and Fridays and the little
text books we use are 'By kind permission of Hugo's phonetic
system'. They also provide us with free tea. [15/6/15].*

The Army was exclusively male and, in the spirit of the age,
women were desperate to be seen to be doing their bit. For the
lower classes this might mean working in a munitions factory,
for the middle classes knitting comforts for the troops, and
for society ladies French lessons and free teas!

The troops seem to have been allowed out every evening
after being stood down from the day's duties. Trips to the
variety theatre were clearly the favourite pastime:

*Still 'in the pink'. I went along with Worswick to Chelsea
Palace last night to see Karno's review* Parlez vous Francais?
Like all Karno's productions it is A1. [27/6/15]

*We went yesterday to Leicester Square and the district is justly
called 'Theatreland', As you walk along you find, almost next
to each other the Apollo, Alhambra, Empire, New, Lyric,
Daly's, Coliseum, Shaftsbury, Globe, Ambassadors and many
others, not to mention picture theatres. As it was we went to
the 'Victoria Palace' and enjoyed it fine, especially Neil Kenyon
with his laughable catchword 'Na-ut-all' spoken very quickly
and meaning 'not at all' [13/6/15]*

Although the real horrors of aerial warfare and blitz bombing were not experienced by Londoners until the Second World War, there was the threat of spasmodic raids by the Zeppelin airships and the newly developed German Taube bombers. The evidence of this danger was all too clear to the lads as they walked back to the barracks after another theatre outing:

We went to Euston varieties last night and the show was excellent. Coming home, about 9.30 p.m., it was very dark and it was wonderful to see the searchlights sweeping the sky with long beams of light which lit up the sky looking for hostile aircraft. [12/6/15]

There were more comprehensive comments about the aerial threat a few weeks later, unwittingly but shrewdly foretelling the attitude of Londoners some twenty-five years later in the Second World War Blitz:

London is all so wonderful to me. There is always something new such as the changing of the Welsh Guards at Buckingham Palace, the daily appearance of balloons over London, the searchlights, the covering of government offices by bomb proof matting etc. [19/7/15]

The darkness greatly accentuates the beams of light which search the heavens for enemy aircraft and it is indeed a pretty spectacle. During the day one can also see the anti-aircraft guns which are over the Admiralty and the War Office. The efficacy of these has to be proved yet but one can imagine the Londoners saying 'we'll do 'em if they come' and if these precautions only give confidence they do good. [19/7/16]

There were also other diversions, such as visits to museums and the National Gallery, where most of the paintings had been removed for fear of Zeppelin raids, and quiet leisure in London's parks:

Today, Sunday, we have spent in Hyde Park, lounging about, and in the afternoon we were rowing on the Serpentine for an hour. Chelsea is a beautiful residential neighbourhood and our headquarters are pleasantly situated and a good band of the Grenadiers plays for about a couple of hours every night [6/6/15]

Willie also explored the possibilities of religion, having only experienced the local Wesleyan chapel in North Street Burnley:

We dropped into the Christian Science room the other night and the librarian, who must have thought me a suitable subject, gave me a short lecture on the religion and asked me to take a few booklets. The book of psalms was pressed on me with the words 'It has been known to give the soldiers much comfort.' [12/6/15]

Yesterday I went to Brompton Oratory for Mass and any new experience I could encounter. It was well worth the trouble, for though the religious service was in no wise as spectacular as I expected, the church interior was as beautiful as anything I have ever seen and the religious movements and mutterings were very strange. In the afternoon the three of us went to the YMCA headquarters in Tottenham Court Road and were there served with a free tea. [21/6/15]

I went to the local YMCA yesterday and the speaker was criticising Blatchford's God is My Neighbour *and it was extremely interesting. He quoted from the text 'Now, if God is all powerful why couldn't he have made the world free of temptation?' He then explained that if there was no wrong there could be no right because one could only do the proper and right thing if there was a wrong thing as an alternative and if we were free from temptation we should have no brain and be nothing more than animals. All very nice, but I think Blatchford was really trying to prove that our will and everything else could not be a product of God. [15/8/15]*

Among the various orders and advice handed out by their officers to the recruits was an interesting one about smoking:

As to cigarettes we are encouraged to give up smoking and on our marches and at lectures only those with pipes are allowed to smoke. [10/6/15]

Clearly there was already some medical awareness about the dangers of smoking cigarettes, probably because of shortage of breath and smokers' coughs rather than the more serious consequences discovered later. Considering that every soldier smoked throughout the war as it was obviously a vital means of relieving stress and that cigarettes were issued free to all troops on active service the above comment is somewhat surprising. Just how important cigarettes were to friend and foe alike is covered more fully in a later chapter.

Willie had smoked from the age of seven, probably like must other boys at the time. He and two friends pooled their Saturday halfpenny spending money to buy a packet of five Woodbine cigarettes for three halfpennies. The three coins were tossed before purchase and the owners of the two which came down on the same side got two cigarettes each while the 'unlucky' third got one cigarette plus the paper sleeve and the cigarette card – the collectable series on favourite subjects which accompanied all brands of cigarettes. There was no law preventing the sale of tobacco to minors!

Another interesting order was that military men were ordered to have short haircuts and were supposed to grow a moustache but not a beard (they were for the Navy). Obviously most young men could not produce anything very quickly, and indeed Willie was not able to grow a moustache until he had been in France for some time. He described the hair on his upper lip as being 'like a cricket match – eleven a side'. The carefully worded instruction ran as follows:

The hair of the head must be kept short and the cheeks and under lip and under chin etc. must be shaved but not the upper lip. [19/7/15]

The recruits had a lecture from one of the doctors about sanitary precautions peculiar to Egypt. This started speculation that they were going to be posted to that country. If they had, they might have been destined to endure the gruelling conditions of the long desert treks of Allenby in the struggle against the Turks. Indeed, the word reached Tom and Bella Whittaker back in Burnley that their son was definitely going to Egypt. The source was unknown but Willie suspected Percy Shoesmith. The truth was:

We are certainly going somewhere before very long for we have had field dressing, extra shoes, a respirator and canvas overalls served out. Rumours are rife but we know absolutely nothing. [2/8/15]

They soon learned that they were destined to move elsewhere in England for more conventional military training and before they left Chelsea for Blackdown Camp in Hampshire the section had a farewell to London party:

Last night we had a sectional night out going to the Victoria Palace review Sugar and Spice *with The three Mears, Jean Schwiller (cello) etc. then went to the Continental restaurant and finished the night off after a good supper with songs, speeches and toasts. [7/8/15]*

The Continental Restaurant was at 7 Wilton Road, London S.W. and the menu for that meal, signed on the back by the comrades who were now regarded as a unit, was enclosed in the letter. The 'good supper' was a five-course dinner! The menu read:

Soup: Sole: Roast Lamb: Ice Cream: Cheese!

The next day they were off to Hampshire to complete their preparation for overseas posting and Willie was billeted with the men who were to be the nucleus of 41st Sanitary Section in Belgium and north-eastern France for the rest of the war.

We left Chelsea this morning at 7 o'clock and proceeded to Waterloo station and thence to Frimley, which is about five miles from Aldershot, where we were met by a transport wagon and guides who took us about four miles through fine country to Blackdown Camp, Farnborough. The camp is finely situated on high ground. After a good dinner we prepared to pitch tents but were saved this trouble by the efforts of our NCOs and were granted two houses (in peacetime married quarters) as billets. I have got on the upper floor with Corporal Lott, Lance Corporal Edwards, Privates Cannon, Mills, Lanigan, Phillips, Bradley and Woolfe. [15/8/15]

The group were pleased to be away from Chelsea and soon had their new billet smartened up and with a few home comforts. They seemed anxious to get into the real war as soon as possible and soon knew that it was not Egypt but to Flanders and north-eastern France that they were going.

As well as being taught field work such as weapon training, semaphore and signalling they carried out sanitary work for the

Brigade they were assigned to for the War Games. Blackdown was principally used for infantry training and must have been a virtual city as the mock action involved enormous numbers of soldiers.

It is interesting to observe that each intake was only at Blackdown for three or four weeks, so the annual total being given their final training at that camp alone before being posted abroad must have been over 100,000 men:

We had orders to parade on Monday in full marching order, with clean shirt and socks wrapped up in our greatcoats. We left Blackdown at 9 o'clock with the 74th Brigade of the 24th Division. The line of men, in fours, stretched for about five miles, there being between seven and ten thousand troops on the road. In between there were travelling field kitchens, where dinner was cooking as we went along. After about three hours marching we halted and the Brigade divided up and placed themselves in various positions on a great moor near Sunningdale. We had a fine hot dinner then pitched three tents where six men slept in each of two of them and the Officers and Staff Sergeant in the other. We then made an incinerator and latrines, urine pit, soakage pit etc. just for our own men and examined and made suggestions on the latrines etc. which were dug for the other men by their respective sanitary squads. 'War' was declared at 4 o'clock and large groups of men moved into the 'trenches'. They were advancing all night and there was no firing until the morning when the Artillery commenced very energetically, making a tremendous roar. Last night we slept on waterproof groundsheets on the bare ground and without exaggeration I have never slept sounder. At the time of writing (10.30 a.m.) we are laid down in the shade in our tent awaiting orders, while on the heights the noise of the Artillery is increasing every moment. We are about three miles from the first line of trenches and are in a similar position to that we shall probably have to take up when we get across. [25/8/15]

After only four weeks at Blackdown, 41st Sanitary Section was on the move to France, almost exactly three months after call up. The great liner *Aquitania*, requisitioned as a hospital ship, was alongside their troopship:

We left Blackdown Camp on Wednesday September 1st at 10 a.m. We marched in broiling sun via Bisley ranges to Brookwood station whence we departed at 10 o'clock for Southampton. Reaching there an hour later we proceeded to one of the large sheds alongside the docks where we stayed until 6.20 when we embarked on the Isle of Man Steam Packet boat Empress Queen. *The docks at Southampton were crowded with transports and hospital ships, amongst which was the* Ellan Vannin *and also the* Aquitania *(a monster hospital ship) and the* Asturias. *We left Southampton at dusk, about 8 o'clock, and sailed through the calm waters of the Solent to the open sea where as far as could be made out in the near darkness we linked up with other transports and a hospital ship, which is always distinguished by being painted white with a red cross in the middle of the hull and two long green lines on either side of the cross, which are illuminated in their respective colours at night. The sea was very choppy and at times exceedingly heavy as the water washed over the decks of the* Empress Queen *and prevented us from having much sleep. Nothing eventful happened during the journey except for a small number of sufferers from 'mal de mer', amongst whom was Bradley, the only man affected in our section. We reached Le Havre pier feeling very jaded and fed up, in pouring rain, at 2.30 on 2 September. [3/9/15]*

Willie had joined a volunteer army and for a long time there was a flood of enthusiasts, patriotically anxious to serve, or at least persuaded to do so by social pressures on every young man to 'do his bit'. For the time being this provided sufficient manpower for the Army. The number and size of the hospital ships must have sent a warning note, however, about the large numbers already, or about to be, wounded at the front.

Later in the war, the slaughter at the battles of Ypres and the Somme made it necessary to introduce conscription on a wide scale to replace those killed and wounded. Men who had failed to volunteer, even in the face of the ostracism epitomised by the sending of the white feather of cowardice, were called up under compulsion. The experience of one such reluctant soldier, Willie's childhood friend Harry Preston, is recounted later.

The pressure on manpower eventually became such that the conscription age was progressively raised to the extent that much older men were called up. Willie's father Tom was still a relatively young man and when the suggestion that men of forty and even older might be compelled to serve, Willie tried to be reassuring in a rather bizarre way. Perhaps his father could join the signalling corps!

Even if the age limit is raised I don't think father will be needed – but, a word in time. There is a soft job in France for older men in charge of pigeon lofts. I have met two Lancashire men in charge of lofts. They must be able to show a fair knowledge of the birds' habits, breeding etc. [17/12/17]

The age limit was indeed raised and call up for Tom became a real possibility:

So at last the silken thread supporting the 'Sword of Damocles' has been severed and father has had his medical inspection. What is the result? I burn to know. Whatever it is, remember these words. Wars are not like streams, they don't go on for ever. [28/5/18]

Thomas Whittaker was not called up after all and in any case it seems that the older recruits were never asked to serve outside Britain. It was obviously sensible to use them in administration or local defence roles to release younger men for the front line.

It must have been with some relief, however, that in 1918, Tom and Bella moved from Lancashire to Cheshire to take up their new duties as 'Mine Hosts' at the George and Dragon public house in Tarvin.

The waiting was over for Willie and he was about to enter the real war at last.

2

On Active Service

During their training in Britain, new recruits, though subject to Army discipline, had a relatively normal life. They had regular hours and well-balanced hot meals during the day, free time in the evenings and decent beds to sleep in at night. This all came to a sudden end on arrival in France.

The younger volunteers were still boys when they enlisted and a life of danger and privation in the war zone soon turned them into men. For William Whittaker and his comrades the contrast between the carefree days of London and Hampshire and the new reality of active service could hardly have been more severe:

Last year at this time I was in England at Blackdown on the threshold of my great adventure. Even at the cost of repetition I do not think it would be amiss to mention the incidents of my twelve months' active service. I was a youth of eighteen years, diving from the springboard of boyhood into the sea of men and life. The long months of horror and experience leave me feeling that I have been robbed of so much youth. [28/10/16]

The rough crossing of the English Channel they had endured was just a foretaste of the horrific journey which was to follow as they moved to the war zone:

We did not leave the ship until 7.30 a.m. before which we had breakfast of bully beef and good hot tea. Marching to another part of the huge docks all our section and many of the Red Cross units that came across with us were put on duty to assist with cleaning and unloading a vessel which had brought a cargo of horses across. We finished this work about noon when we marched off to a 'rest' camp about two miles from the docks, where many troops were billeted. We fixed up eleven in each tent and then had dinner of more bully and biscuits. We left the camp at midnight with the weather still bad. [5/9/15]

Things were worse the next day:

We reached the railway station after marching through inches of mud at about 1.30 a.m. All the town was in absolute darkness so I had no opportunity of seeing what Le Havre was like. We were packed in cattle trucks and told we were going straight to the front. Commencing our journey at about 5.00 a.m. some of us managed to snatch a few hours' sleep on the damp floor of the truck. We passed through Yvetot, Rouen, Amiens and Montreuil to Mareschel where we arrived at about 7.30 p.m. Meals all day have been bully and biscuits. We reached a farm owned by the mayor of the district at about 10.00 p.m. and slept in a barn.

Rising at 6.00 a.m. I had a very necessary shave and wash and then hung about and between meals ate apples, which grow in profusion around here. Our lorry arrived at about 7.00 p.m. and brought us all English cigarettes just when we were running short, also bringing us blankets etc. At 9 o'clock I undressed for the first time in three days and slept. The next morning we had bacon for breakfast and I think bacon was never so tasty before – a pleasant change after nothing but bully beef for several days. [5/9/15]

After this first experience of life on active service the section enjoyed a few quiet weeks. A year later he wrote home recalling what had happened on that fateful journey from rural England to the war zone. It is interesting to contrast what actually happened, so graphically described in gruesome detail above, to his later memory of it, which does not quite agree in all details:

We sailed at dusk in the Empress Queen. *We were off to France. What should we do there? To what part should we go? Should we be troubled with sickness and death? All these and many more questions were stirring in my brain before we had been aboard an hour. We reached Le Havre at 2 a.m., chilled and wet and tired. We helped to unload other transports and spent the night fourteen in a hut in a Rest Camp and then our train journey to Maraschel. We walked in the dark to Beaunainville, carrying along roads swimming in mud three or four 50 lb. boxes of biscuits in turn. We billeted in a barn and I laid down to sleep without stripping a single thing.*

We spent some happy days at Beaunainville. It was novel to be in the midst of a different speaking race with different customs, dress and habitation. The people were all farmers and lived off the land and by the land. Mother earth in war and peace does not change the production of a crop of potatoes or wheat or apples. We were about the first English soldiers who had been in that district and our welcome and treatment was therefore of the best. They trusted us in their orchards and we did not take more apples than they wished. [30/10/16]

The section had not after all been sent straight to the front but at the beginning of November 1915 the idyllic life at Beaunainville came to an abrupt end with a gruesome journey to the war zone:

To look back on what has happened since I came to France makes me wonder how I passed through it all. We left X at 2.30 one afternoon to march to Y, a distance of six miles. We little thought how tremendously irksome our sixty pound pack would be before we could take it off. Leaving Y after tea at 6 o'clock in a mile long column we commenced at a rattling pace on a steep uphill march. We struggled on, hour after hour. Darkness set in, the moon rose and when a halt was given nearly everybody dropped in his tracks, careless of the very thick dust and dirt which coated the roads. How worn out we were. Off again! trudge, trudge, trudge, with burning feet, tickling throat and aching shoulders and backs caused by the heavy packs. As we moved along we would often pass (more and more towards the end) one or two who sat down at the roadside, having dropped down in their tracks, absolutely incapable of marching another foot. At times I almost felt the same. We reached Z at about 1.30 a.m. dead beat and the only accommodation that we had was some old pig sties, the floors of which were rough cobbles that protruded in some cases to quite three inches above the level of the floor. Oh agony! And yet we slept, tired as we were. We lay all day out in the sun, still tired and sore and at 6 o'clock we were off again. Very soon three of our chaps had fallen out and later on two or three were taking turns to ride on the accompanying ambulances. I stuck that march too and when we had a foot parade the day after I was the only one whose feet did not require attention. We finished that march at 4.00 a.m. [1/11/15]

Just what madness prompted this kind of manoeuvre is not explained and the victims could not even make a surmise as to why they were subjected to such torment because it would have fallen foul of the censor. One can understand why the marches in the war zone were carried out in darkness as otherwise the columns could have been targets for shelling, but why the troops should be driven to a point where they all needed foot medication and were totally unfit to carry out any task, let alone fight, is inexplicable. What a welcome to the front!

Of course, the officers who accompanied the march would all be on horseback and they would not have slept in pigsties. They were no doubt themselves ordered by more senior officers from their desks in comfortable headquarter chateaux to push the men to their physical limit in some sort of demonstration of how tough the British Tommy was. In spite of it all, Tommy remained cheerful:

Some of the songs sung during the marches were rather amusing, if a little rude – e.g. 'When this b—y war is over, no more soldiering for me' to the tune of 'Take me to the lord n prayer' and many others of the same stamp. [2/11/15]

After these marches we were fortunately allowed to journey with a convoy of motor ambulances and even that was not all beer and skittles. On one occasion we were left huddled uncomfortably with knees up to our chins from 8.00 p.m. to 4.00 a.m. during a wet and bitterly cold night. Our shelter from 4.00 a.m. was a shippon, where we slept near the cows. [3/11/15]

In spite of all the pain of this 'advance', Willie was able to reflect, in his usual philosophical way, about a moving incident on the march which demonstrated the cheerfulness of Tommy and his willingness to get on with the job of defeating the enemy under conditions of the greatest adversity:

I never regret joining up. On the contrary, my only regret is that you would not let me join a line regiment for I felt that I was only half doing my duty when I saw the wounded passing the other day during our long advance. One 'Jock', who was seemingly wounded from head to toe judging from his bandages, was sitting on the back step of an ambulance with a German helmet on his head and a Woodbine cigarette in his mouth. He answered all enquiries with a cheerful:

'Hurry up lads, it's a b—y walkover. There won't be a b-gg-r left if you don't hurry.'

Could you wish for a better example of British humour in the face of death. I think the Jocks are our best fighters. They refused to leave the trenches on one occasion and when they were relieved there were only seventeen left of a whole company of two hundred and fifty men. Of course, this is fortunately an exceptional circumstance. [2/11/15]

This all took place before the horrendous battles of Ypres, Passchendale and the Somme, where such casualties would have been described as 'slight' in official reports.

In the same letter Willie contrasts the British Army at home and the British Army at war by describing the former as a 'holiday' and the latter as 'damned hard graft'. Accepting the naïve assumption that the war would soon be over, he did not realise that he would be in France for four years!

Yes, the boys certainly grew up into men – and seasoned soldiers – very, very quickly.

3

Health and Hygiene

The 1914–1918 war was the first major conflict in which professional attention to sanitation by trained specialists was used, with hugely successful results. Disease from lack of hygiene became a rarity for the first time. As a result countless lives were saved.

The basic elements of the work of the sanitary sections of the Royal Army Medical Corps were to ensure safe drinking water supplies, regular body-washing, delousing, provision of latrines, elimination of insects and waste disposal. A variety of techniques were used, from the building of incinerators to contraptions for ensuring that the seats of latrines were closed. Some of these devices were illustrated in official documents and sketches of some were included in the letters, while the incinerators, which could burn almost anything, were so successful that giant ones were built by the Army to serve whole towns.

Educated young volunteers were eagerly accepted into the sanitary service by the authorities and although most of them bore the rank of Private throughout the war, they had very considerable authority over the areas of their responsibility. William Whittaker was one of those who volunteered for the RAMC and was readily accepted at the age of eighteen without query about his age.

The men who were to be the nucleus of the 41st Sanitary Section came together at Chelsea Barracks and later at Blackdown. They remained comrades, with occasional additions, for the rest of the war. They were privates Whittaker, Cannon, Lanigan, Woolfe, Phillips, Law, Marfleet and Bradley, with Corporal Lott and Lance Corporal Edwards.

Shortly after their arrival in Flanders the opportunity arose for Willie to be selected for a desk job, which would have meant a safe location at some headquarters. Although his work at the county court would have equipped him for such a post, his eagerness to be involved in the real war caused him to spurn this possibility. The desire to feel that one was really 'doing one's bit' was so prevalent that men cheerfully went forward to the battle zone with all its danger and risk of wounding or death:

The officer has spoken to all clerks in the section. They may possibly, if desired, be given clerking duties in various places. We are to tell him in the morning what we desire to do. I do not think I shall make any effort to acquire one of these jobs for they will very likely be stationary and I want to see more, even at a little discomfort. [7/12/15]

A variety of tasks awaited the eager young man, some relatively safe and easy, others much more dangerous:

Fortunately my present occupation is far from arduous. I am stationed with the section at X and am in charge of some water tanks nearby. The village is, I dare say, the only one so near the Germans that has not suffered demolition. [25/5/16]

My present work takes me daily to places less than a thousand yards from our front line trench. I approach these places along communications trenches. I am in charge of the sanitary arrangements of what was once a model village now situated on the edge of the trenches. It must have been a wonderfully pretty place but it now makes a desolate, pathetic scene, with its trampled gardens, torn fences and battered houses. Fortunately, the line here is rather quiet and with an ordinary amount of care one is quite safe. [1/11/16]

Sergeant Dennis, Cannon and I are daily in charge of gangs of German prisoners performing elementary sanitary work, burying and burning refuse and generally clearing up. The prisoners are very docile and on the whole work well. [22/12/17]

I still on various days work with German prisoners. There is a distinct change in their appearance and they are looking very much better than they did a few weeks ago. This is splendid testimony to our treatment and feeding of prisoners of war. They work well and are scrupulously obedient as behoves them. There are some very young boys amongst them and one cannot help but feel just a teeny bit sorry for them. Just a teeny bit for collectively I hate these Germans, with an understandable hate. So many of them look so brutal. They have a cast of countenance which is so typically German and if only for this I hate them. [15/1/18]

Towards the end of the war, in 1918, most of the original group were given acting rank of Lance Corporal, though Willie had to wait for his promotion even though he was to end up as a full Corporal and acting Sergeant. The possible reason for the late promotion and an amusing incident was described thus:

I told you a few months ago that all the section (with the exception of about seven of us) were given acting rank of Lance Corporal. Your humble servant (for reasons it is perhaps not wise to proclaim) was not included in this lavish distribution of promotion. Nevertheless I still carry on with the same work as heretofore and bear the same duties and responsibilities of the chosen ones, who in all conscience have no satisfaction from and can show little gratitude for their embellishment.

A rather amusing dialogue took place a few days ago between the officer and Lance Corporal Johnson in the workshop:

Officer: Johnson, why were these men not called to attention?

Johnson: I forgot about it sir.

Officer (angrily): Do you know the duties of an NCO?

Johnson: Yes sir.

Officer: What are they?

Johnson: To call the men to attention sir. [7/7/18]

It could be that Willie's delayed promotion was because of a black mark on his record when he had broken the rules about what was not allowed to be included in letters home. He had been hauled before the censor for an indiscretion, an incident which is described in a later chapter.

As well as the tasks outlined above, the sanitary section was even required to supervise street cleaning when a VIP was visiting, especially when the visitor was King George V himself!

I still retain my road cleaning foreman's job and if I continue long enough I shall begin to consider myself an expert on the work. The King, General French and the Prince of Wales have been here today, walked along the troop-lined road and inspected the men. Previous to their arrival the roads had to be cleaned and I was called to assist the authorities to decide how many men and carts would be needed. Some duty! Two hundred men and five carts were employed and all was nice and clear when His Majesty arrived. [27/10/15]

Willie soon moved on to more normal duties including the construction of a variety of devices, some fairly crude but all effective, the usual latrines and incinerators but also ablution benches, meat safes and refuse bins. The section workshop must have been a busy place, relatively well equipped with tools and materials. The section was also serviced by its own motor transport:

Each section has a motor lorry and the tackle we carry in them must be worth some money. There are two wheelbarrows, steam disinfectors for field use (quite expensive, bulky and interesting things), water clarifier, fifty groundsheets, blankets, tents, flagpoles, picks, shovels, axes, carpenters outfit, saddlery, disinfectant, sprays, collapsible lanterns etc. [15/8/15]

I am now erecting incinerators of a more or less permanent type, along with Black and Babb. The work gives one a chance of seeing much of the district. A destructor has been, is being, or will be constructed on the camp of practically every unit of any size in the division. They are brick erections consisting of four walls about nine inches thick, around five and a half feet high and about five feet square. In one wall there are two doors, one above the other. The incinerator is fed through the high one and cleared through the lower. On top of the walls is a sheet of iron with a six foot chimney through it, or rather protruding from it. These destructors have a strong draught and if fed sensibly will burn practically anything. They are being used to burn latrine refuse so you will perhaps realise their necessity during the summer in a district where practically all the ground is foul and not fit for burning excreta. [13/5/16]

The section made fifteen of these destructors in various camps, each of which could burn the refuse from a camp of 1,000 men. Willie described the work, which involved the laying of thousands of bricks for each destructor, as the hardest physical work he had ever undertaken, but he also records how fit he was becoming and how he was 'in the pink'. They were also called upon to build even bigger ones to serve whole towns:

Your humble, with several others, has been fixing a large chimney to the town destructor. Altogether we were faced with a formidable task. I was placed with another man at the point where the chimney met the roof of the building with no support other than my own limbs and it was our business to see that the chimney did not slide at its base when it was being raised. When the chimney was at an angle it slipped at the base and how we avoided a heavy fall is due to the others who acted in time and dragged the chimney back. [9/10/16]

Latrines were a magnet for insects and a novel way of encouraging proper use of latrine seats was devised:

To checkmate the fly pest it is essential that the lids on latrine seats are shut down after they have been used. Tommy is a little careless of these details and many are our efforts to enforce this precaution. One is to put a support which will catch the lid when opened and, by keeping it at an angle, will cause it to fall shut under its own weight when not in use. Under rough usage however this idea is soon useless so we struck on another idea of putting a notice board where the soldiers couldn't fail to see it thus: HAVE YOU CLOSED THE LID. The sign has been much praised but I think the latest idea by our officer goes one better. It plays on the curiosity of the user and should be successful if for that fact only. The lid, when opened, shows on the underside – PTO. Who can resist turning it over and incidentally shutting the lid. On the other side is the image of a fly and the words: KEEP IT DOWN. [7/7/18]

The dangers posed by the fly menace and one of the more amusing and devastatingly effective ways of dealing with it was described thus:

The fly trouble has multiplied enormously. Diarrhoea has been prevalent but cases have been immediately dosed and beyond discomfort there has been nothing very serious. I was at a camp today where the occupants have concocted a novel fly killer. They drop some jam or meat on to the floor and make a circle of cordite round it. When the flies are settled in full strength down goes a match and – there you are – five hundred casualties. If we could only tempt the Germans with a bit of jam or meat ... ! [5/9/16]

The manure from the vast numbers of horses, required mainly for hauling weapons and transport, also created fly problems:

In the narrow stretch of land behind the front there are hundreds of thousands of horses and consequently colossal quantities of horse manure. The French people nearby have taken advantage of this stock of fine fertiliser and the result can be seen in the land round about, but the French have not taken enough of it to prevent us having to worry our heads about its disposal. It is, as you know, a very popular breeding place for flies and there are many methods in practice to prevent the multiplication of these dangerous insects. Manure is burned if possible and where impossible it is stacked in large heaps, tightly compressed and sprayed with disinfectant daily. [28/5/17]

Perhaps the most important of all the tasks required of the section was the safety and continuity of water supplies. Sometimes it was hard physical work but at other times a very soft job:

The boys are situated at some huge water tanks where they fill more than a hundred carts a day. The water is drawn from a lake near Dickebush. This lake runs off into the trenches and therefore the water supply requires careful supervision. [21/1/16]

I am at Dranoutre now, working on a water supply and am having a wonderfully easy time. [20/5/16]

Bodily hygiene was also all-important and regular showers and a change of clothing were arranged wherever possible:

Along with Sergeant Dennis, Kilburn, Cannon and Bradley I am helping to construct a huge filtering arrangement to deal with the dirty and soapy water from the baths and laundry attached thereto. It is hard work of a manual nature and I now feel so well that I quite enjoy the rather vigorous exercise. We saw up enormous quantities of wood which is constructed into very large watertight tanks; this is accomplished by tar and strips of blanket in every crack. [27/4/16]

The baths consist of an undressing room and the bath proper. The bather hands his suit of khaki to an attendant, who takes it to be ironed and fumigated. He also hands in his dirty underclothing for which he receives a wood or metal tag. If shirt and a pair of pants are handed in a red tag is given and if shirt, pants and socks, a green tag. The bather during this time is naked and as soon as possible makes for the bath. To save water five or six bathers crowd under the shower and the water is turned on full for ten seconds. It is hot water. The water is then turned down to a mere trickle when one is supposed to soap oneself. This takes two or three minutes then the water is turned back on for another ten seconds to wash the soap away. Not much of a bath, but it is something to be thankful for and even looked forward to. After bathing one goes back to the dressing room, dries himself and hands in his tag at the clothing store where he receives clean duplicates of the stuff he gave in dirty. By the time he has donned these his khaki has been cleaned and the business is over. It does not take more than twenty minutes. [4/4/17]

The bathing and laundering, apart from for the obvious removal of dirt, was particularly important for the extermination of body lice. Although only referred to in one letter, Willie recalled that when ironing one's own clothes there was a tell tale 'pop' when a louse went under the heat. He also remembered the rather cynical attitude of one of his comrades, who always put a live louse back in his clothing to make sure that any survivors would have company.

I look forward to having a bath every morning when I come home on leave. I have known what it is to be 'lousy' and admit that one never feels clean out here. [9/3/16]

I wonder how many people nowadays realise when using the everyday term 'lousy', meaning something pretty bad, that it actually derives from the parasitical creatures that infested every Tommy in France.

The section had to be mobile and their various billets, some fairly comfortable, some bizarre and some awful are described later. When they went up the line, however, they lived underground in dugouts:

Your query whether I am likely to be sent up the line again is noted. Yes, most certainly, I will be up there again. You see, we work a set of reliefs for the line and single men usually do this work. There are about eight or ten of us who change about. No man is ever up the line unaccompanied. Black and Johnson are now in a mining town which Fritz held until a few weeks ago. [16/5/17]

Most of the time 41st Section was stationed just behind the line exposed to shelling, gas and aerial bombing. They were a lucky section and spells in the trenches were not frequent, but others were not so fortunate:

I can assure you that it is much more exceptional than usual for members of my section to visit the front line. Some sanitary sections are often there and have had many casualties, but we have had the devil's luck. [9/10/16]

Nevertheless, they had to serve in the trenches sometimes. One session there demonstrated just how dangerous this could be and how lucky 41st Section was:

More than half of us are now living in dugouts. The section which we have relieved is, I think, the most unfortunate sanitary section in the field. Out of their twenty odd men they have lost, since coming out here, about eleven men by death, wounds and sickness. [13/8/16]

The relatively safe life of the RAMC men drew cynical remarks from the infantry, who spent much of their time in the line:

Sergeant Gooding and Corporal Lanigan had an exciting and unexpected experience a few days ago when they had to go to the front line trenches for disinfecting purposes and each of them says he felt quite safe whilst up there but terribly nervous en route. For some distance they had to cross open ground practically in sight of the enemy who often cover this particular part with machine gun and shell fire. Whilst up there they were subject to many sarcastic remarks. One of the 'Blankshires' turned to his pal and said in tones of astonishment 'Fancy Bill, two blinking Red Cross blokes in the front line'. Corporal Lanigan was very much amused at a notice on top of the trench which said 'Spring Gardens'. It was in the middle of a wire enclosure in which grew one daisy. [25/5/16]

The sanitary engineers were never called upon to 'go over the top' like the infantrymen, whose lives were squandered in so many futile attacks, although they were exposed to all the other dangers of warfare. There were also what would today be called 'industrial accidents', one of which claimed the life of a colleague in Willie's section during the erection of an incinerator:

A very unfortunate accident on Sunday resulted in the death of one of our attached men, a young fellow called Davies. He and two others were building an incinerator so as to burn a quantity of refuse and in their ignorance fixed a grid which consisted of hollow iron bars full of a certain very powerful explosive. The fire was lit, poor Davies was killed and his Corporal was badly injured. The third man escaped, suffering from shock. [28/11/17]

That the work done by the sanitary sections was recognised by the highest authorities was evidenced by the praise handed out:

Corporal Edwards and I are on duty at the General's headquarters. I have been on this duty for over three months now and have been praised for doing the work well. You will understand that, above all, the sanitary conditions in and around HQs must be absolutely 'it'. We always have about eight fatigues and do no actual manual labour ourselves. [1/4/16]

Sir Douglas Haig's report reads – 'All branches of the medical service deserve the highest commendation for the successful work done by them both at the front line and along the lines of communication. The sick rate has been consistently low, there has been no serious epidemic or enteric fever. The losses of armies in the past have almost disappeared owing to preventative measures energetically carried out'. [3/5/16]

A divisional order revealed that although each division had a sanitary section attached to it, the latter did not move with the division but remained in the same area. No doubt this was because local expertise about water supplies and other installations was too valuable to lose. The order read:

On leaving the 41st sanitary section in its permanent area the divisional commander wishes to place on record his high appreciation of the services rendered by this unit during the eighteen months that it has formed part of the division overseas. All ranks appreciate the quality of the work done by the section. Signed General …x… [29/4/17]

This week our work has been inspected by several heads of the Medical Services, including Generals, and they are all very satisfied that we are very actively doing our bit. Further honour is done to our section by our Staff Sergeant being mentioned in dispatches. We are proud of our good work and grateful that the head men have said leave will be granted as liberally as possible. [3/6/17]

The hints at leave were really empty words. Leave was always subject to the workload of the section and overriding all were the exigencies of war which led to all leave being cancelled when an offensive was planned. Willie had few illusions about the above words, while still remaining optimistic that the war would soon be over.:

Despite this news I am very pessimistic with regard to my own chances of leave. I do not expect to see you until 'après la guerre' unless the war lasts over another winter. I do not think it will last that long although to read the papers you would think otherwise. [3/6/17]

The authorities were so proud of the equipment produced by and for the sanitary sections that they created museums to display them. This equipment was not only used in France, as Willie's lifelong friend John Kippax, who had volunteered for the RAMC with him, was posted to Salonica. One of John's surviving letters to his old schoolmate described some of the specialist equipment used in the hotter climate of Salonica where mosquitoes were a serious problem. The letter mentioned that a museum had been set up there as well.

Both Willie and John had their share of the horrors of war – John refusing to relate the dreadful events he had experienced in Salonica throughout the rest of his long life. The good work of the Sanitary Service, which must have saved tens of thousands of lives, did, however, give them the satisfaction of knowing that they had more than done their bit. Willie never repeated the rather guilty feeling he had expressed in the early letter written from Flanders, when he witnessed wounded troops returning from the front line, that he wished his parents had encouraged him to join an infantry regiment.

Service in the RAMC was only slightly less dangerous than in the infantry and the contribution to the war effort, and its eventual success was surely at least as great as that of most ordinary soldiers.

4

Comrades

It seems incredible nowadays in the light of our knowledge of the slaughter and carnage of the First World War that even among troops at the front there was a genuine patriotic feeling that '*Dulce et decorum est pro patria mori*', and men faced death rather than dishonour. To be sure, desertion or failure to go into battle when ordered to do so could and did in many tragic cases lead to the death penalty, executed by one's own side. The overwhelming majority had no thought of any form of cowardice and followed their young officers 'over the top' in the face of a hail of machine-gun bullets, intent on making an advance and killing as many Germans as they could in the process.

Overriding all this, however, was a much more immediate and powerful influence: the spirit of comradeship and above all the desire not to let down one's fellow men. Medal citations are full of incidents of personal heroism as men attempted to rescue wounded colleagues, often resulting in their own death or injury.

The authorities were clearly aware of the significance of these local bonds and to strengthen what was in any case a very powerful human motivation, deliberately formed regiments on geographical lines, usually named after counties or regions of Britain, or including 'Scots' or 'Irish' in their names. Even within regiments the men from a certain town were often kept together in units. One such unit, part of the East Lancashire Regiment, from Accrington, a town only a few miles from Burnley, named themselves 'The Accrington Pals' and went down in the folklore of the war after being almost wiped out.

The Sanitary Service could not be formed on regional lines, being made up of educated volunteers from all parts of the country. The 41st Section was made up of men from all over England and the nucleus came together right at the start of their service, firstly at Chelsea Barracks and then in field training in Hampshire. The bond of comradeship was as strong as if they had known each other from boyhood. The names of these and others who joined them read like a list of the Huntingdonshire cabmen of E. H. Morton (Beachcomber of the *Daily Express*).

Mills, Phillips, Babb. Black, Marfleet, Law, Cannon, Chisnall, Johnson, Bradley, Lanigan, Phillips, Messent, Smith, Woolfe, Salter and of course Whittaker. The men never used first names; it was always surnames, nicknames or abbreviations – used familiarly and with the usual banter of men thrown together in a common cause.

Willie, as he was always known to his parents, was never called that by his comrades. It seems that a letter from Johnson, written to Tom and Bella Whittaker when he was on leave, had referred to their son as 'Will':

I am sorry to have to dash your illusions as to the members of the section calling me 'Will'. Johnson's use of that name in his letter to you is the first time I remember being referred to as 'Will' by anyone except my sincere Lancashire chum Bradley. No, I am usually addressed as 'Whitt' or more familiarly as 'Old Bill'. After all, 'What's in a name?' as Shakespeare said. Everybody's name in the section is altered in some way. Bradley is 'Brad', Mills is 'Sambo', Cannon is 'Joey', Woolfe is 'Nigger', Percy Kilburn is called 'Pete', John Law is called 'Jimmy', Chisnall becomes 'Chizz', Marfleet is 'Marrowfat', Johnson is 'Johnnie', Smith is 'Erb', Babb is 'Dido', Sadler is 'Archie' and Phillips becomes 'Phil'. I cannot explain many of these names but they are invariably used. [10/7/17]

Many of the comrades were 'characters' – Woolfe the timid, Bradley the orator, Mills the pessimist etc. Willie commented on some of these traits:

As you will have gathered from previous letters, my gifted friend Bradley is our champion orator. This is easily understood when I mention that he is descended from a line of Methodists and his forefathers have been preachers and Parish Clerks of Ribchester for countless years. Yes, dear old Brad is some youth and though of parson stock his views are socialist and agnostic.

Sambo Mills dolefully asserts that the Rumanian muddle has put another three years on the war. He is a big, hefty chap and to quote Bradley 'He is the contradiction of all my

previous ideas that body and brain can grow together'. These words of Bradley's are rich in humour when you consider his own small stature. It is perhaps because of Mills's deep reading of war news that brings on him the opprobrium 'pessimist'.
[3/12/16]

Willie kept in touch with his old childhood friends throughout the war. He kept up a regular correspondence with his old form mate at Burnley Grammar School, John Kippax, and Harry Preston.

His relationship with Harry Preston throws a fascinating light on the patriotic attitudes of the serving soldiers and the contempt of civilians for those who did not volunteer to fight.

Harry Preston and William Whittaker became boyhood friends through their musical talent. Harry was a very fine pianist and Willie was a highly competent violinist. The two boys played duets together and performed at church fairs and other social events in Burnley.

Whereas Willie volunteered for the Army as soon as he dared in 1915, a year underage, Harry did not and presumably hoped that conscription would not be put in force in what, at that time, was expected to be a short war.

The pressures on young men to volunteer were, however, very real and those who did not became increasingly regarded as dodgers who were shirking their duty by letting others fight and die to preserve everybody's freedom while also keeping the nation's honour in maintaining international alliances intact.

It became common practice to serve these men with the 'white feather' of cowardice, and whether or not Harry Preston received this symbolic accusation, it was certain that his reluctance to join up was well known to people in Burnley, including Tom and Bella Whittaker. They evidently kept Willie informed about the situation with his old friend, who had appealed against his conscription when service became compulsory a few months after Willie had joined up. Willie's reaction sums up just how strong were the feelings provoked by someone's failure to 'do his bit'. Ties of upbringing and even the closest of friendships were, at least temporarily, sacrificed in light of the common cause. Willie had just received a letter from Thomas Sutcliffe, an old mentor of his at Sunday school in Burnley and an uncle of Harry Preston and his brother Jerry, when he wrote home with the following bitter recrimination of Jerry and the reluctant Harry:

In his letter Sutcliffe said that Harry's brother Jerry Preston had returned from camp and that he was not sorry to leave the 'rabble'. He also said that Harry was still practicing piano with Uncle Jim. However his letter was such that I am afraid I let my thoughts run away with me in my reply. I said that though Jerry's temporary 'mates' were to him 'rabble' I know from experience that they were men. I cannot remember all my reply but I know that Harry Preston was in my mind's eye all the time I was writing and that it made me rather angry to read of him practicing as usual (and incidentally living and enjoying home comforts as usual) whilst the 'rabble' were fighting courageously and dying bravely. Altogether his letter took the form of a sneer at brave soldiers and I answered it as such. I have since been lucky to receive no further communication from that source.

I feel that Harry Preston will not be remembered among my acquaintances, we will have been 'never friends' after this dreadful war is finished. [21/2/16]

Conscription did catch up with Harry, but this news did not soften Willie's feelings at first:

I am very surprised that that fellow Preston's appeal has been of no avail and I sincerely hope that his army life will be difficult and arduous. [13/5/16]

By October 1916 Harry had done his basic training and was on active service in France and the ties of friendship showed signs of returning:

If you send me Harry Preston's address I may send him a line. I should like to meet him out here. Now that he is doing his share reconciliation is possible. [9/10/16]

Harry certainly did have it 'difficult and arduous'. He had to join the infantry – no possibility of an educated conscripted boy applying for a more interesting and perhaps safer job as early volunteers had been able to do. The next reference to him in the letters comes only two months later. Harry had been 'over the top' into the teeth of enemy fire and was wounded. It is not clear what the injury was, though it was evidently quite severe, but not a 'Blighty' wound, as Harry was hospitalised in France:

I have had a letter from Harry Preston today and he appears to be catching it very rough. He writes from a field hospital and tells me that he feels as weak as a kitten. He says 'no more strength have I than a child and at times I feel positively helpless'. I am very sorry that he is in this state and it is unfortunate that his new address has been censored and consequently I cannot send him a line. [19/12/16]

On return to his unit Harry was not put back in the line and got a soft number of a job:

I received a letter from Harry Preston yesterday. He has now left the base and I quote: 'I was much surprised to find myself in a re-conquered city in last summer's advanced area. Today I have been given a job and of all the work there is in the Army I don't think you would ever guess what it is. I am now the Assistant Chaplain's general orderly. My duties comprise taking messages, lighting fires etc. I think Preston is very lucky don't you? [16/4/17]

Willie's comments encapsulate a feeling commonly expressed by those who had been exposed to enemy fire and not been killed; the luckiest ones were not the unharmed survivors but those who had been injured severely enough to be withdrawn from the front line. There were many who actually wished for a 'Blighty' wound so serious that they would be safely evacuated back to Britain – even missing one or more limbs!

The two friends, now clearly reconciled, kept in regular touch. Harry had a leave just before the Armistice and Willie wrote to him afterwards saying how he would have been welcome at a hostelry of their acquaintance, where Harry would have been invited to 'rattle the dominos'.

As did most young men, Willie and Harry enjoyed a pint of beer and the reference to a favourite pub foreshadowed regular later contact. The story of the two musical friends has a happy ending. Harry took up a professional career as musical director at the Victoria Theatre in Burnley, where he conducted a small orchestra from the piano for music hall shows, plays, pantomimes etc. Willie worked about 12 miles away in the industrial town of Barnoldswick, where he was manager of the local branch of Martins Bank. He visited his widowed mother Bella in Rosegrove, a suburb of Burnley, every second Saturday throughout the football season. His routine was to watch the home fixtures of Burnley in the football league. He would then go to Rosegrove for a meal with his mother, timing a return to Burnley to coincide with the interval between the first and second houses at the Victoria Theatre, where there were two shows every Saturday evening. In the half-hour between the shows he and Harry slipped in to the local pub behind the theatre and enjoyed a couple of pints of beer.

This arrangement went on for at least a couple of decades, and the writer remembers it well that for about ten of those years he accompanied his father on the trips to watch football and to see his grandma, where there was always a treat of fish and chips. While his father and 'Uncle' Harry went to the pub, young Geoffrey was looked after by 'Auntie' Esther, Harry's wife, who played first violin in the theatre band. This involved going backstage with its exciting smell of greasepaint and the glamour of seeing the artists up close. The greatest treat of all was to be allowed to watch the first part of the second show from the wings of the stage before catching a late bus back home.

Willie's relationship with his other boyhood friend, John Kippax, is covered in more detail elsewhere. John was, by a few months, the older of the two, but they volunteered together, John not needing to lie about his age. His call up was slightly delayed, or he might have served in France. Instead he was sent to Salonica. This was an interesting excerpt from one of John's letters:

Our greatest task in this country is our anti-malarial work which goes on all the year round. The summer campaign though is really hard work. We have large gangs of civilian labourers in our different areas, all marshes drained, streams channelled, ponds coated with oil and all undergrowth near water cut and burnt periodically. [21/2/18]

The friends met in France in 1919 when John was on his way home for demobilisation, holidayed together in Paris after the war, as civilians, and were to become brothers-in-law, maintaining a close relationship for another fifty years.

Other childhood friends with whom Willie corresponded included Gilbert Faulds and Donald Kay:

I met Donald Kay just one week before he left our district and it was a great disappointment to both of us to have had such a short time together. May we soon meet again in the more congenial and salubrious atmosphere of Blighty. I have since come across another Burnley fellow, Ben Witham, who is serving with the Canadian 'Canucks' but plumps for England as his domicile after the war. Ben hopes to be home on leave shortly and has promised to call on Uncle James. [26/9/17]

The enthusiastic support between members of the section pervades the entire correspondence – for example:

Kilburn has been awarded the Meritorious Service Medal which we all agree he thoroughly deserves. He is a gold medallist in building and joinery and is so clever in his work that in civilian life he is an instructor of the Allied Arts in Sheffield. He is a wonderfully capable man and his ideas and craftsmanship have brought much credit to the section. [30/10/16]

Willie was equally positive about the skills of men serving alongside him in other units:

One of my acquaintances is Sergeant Symonds of the Buffs. He is an excellent violin player and before the war was the leading violinist in the Viceroy of India's orchestra. Corporal Flowers is a fellow of the Royal College of Organists and I was delightfully entertained by his performance of some of Chopin's works for the piano in the canteen the other night. One meets clever fellows out here.

Speaking of army acquaintances I have met fellows I shall never forget and to whom I will be sorry to say goodbye. There is Merriton of the Staffs who is one of the most witty and entertaining conversationalist I have ever met. In civil life he is the Vicar of Westbourne and a Bachelor of Arts. He seldom speaks of religious matters and is a real good sort who likes the light French beer and is not ashamed to say so. He is a Private earning fourteen pence a day and were his character different he would no doubt have been a chaplain earning £1 a day. [11/19/16]

The war comrades were from all parts of the country, and strong though the bonds were, it was typical of this kind of transient friendship that they would not survive the war. Willie never kept in touch with any of them except briefly with 'Brad' Bradley after demobilisation. That he ever forgot them is unlikely, but he never mentioned them to the knowledge of his family.

One letter from Bradley, who returned to work in his father's road haulage business, survives. It strikes a wistful note about his relationship with a girl he had known as a child. She seems to have claimed him as a future husband and Bradley appears to have been anything but happy about the arrangement, though accepting the liaison as inevitable. There was a desperate imbalance between the sexes after the war as so many men had been killed in action, and many women were left as spinsters for life as a result. It is not surprising that Bradley's girlfriend was not about to let him go!

The friendships that were for life were those of childhood – Harry and John.

5

Censorship

Correspondence between the soldiers and their parents, wives, other relatives and friends was not only an important link with home but also a comfort which made life at the front bearable. It helped morale and provided a routine task which brought some order into unpredictable lives.

The troops were issued with standard envelopes – small, plain and green in colour. These were sent back to Britain free of charge but, although issued fairly liberally, they were rationed.

Letters from 'other ranks' were subject to censorship. Any letter not in an official envelope was automatically censored, while 'greens', as they were affectionately known, were subject to random censorship. Letters written by officers were not censored. The rules on censorship were strict and the underlying principle was that nothing should be included that might lower morale on the home front. Additionally, anything, however trivial, that might be of assistance to the enemy was also banned, even including simple references as to where the writer was.

One form of correspondence which was not censored was the field postcard. This was a pre-printed card with statements that could be crossed out where inappropriate to convey simple messages. These served two purposes. The first was for those who could not read and write, for there was still a fair amount of illiteracy, and the second for anyone who, because of the pressures of the service, including actual fighting, or simply lack of time, could not write a proper letter.

The postcards read:

'I am quite well'
'I have been admitted into Hospital' (sick) (wounded)
'and am going on quite well'
'and hope to be discharged soon'
'I have received your' (letter dated) (telegram) (parcel)
'Letter follows at first opportunity'
'I have received no letter from you' (lately) (for a long time)

There was space for signature and date, but in heavy type was printed '**If anything else is added this post card will be destroyed.**'

Censorship produced a sort of reverse propaganda so that no news of mass slaughter, lack of territory gained by armies bogged down in trenches, or 'leaks' about new campaigns could offset the official line published in the British press, which was invariably optimistic.

Although no doubt planned with the best intentions, the authorities could not prevent real news about the war being disseminated by soldiers on their rare home leaves, not only to their own circle but also through clandestine notes posted or passed directly to the relatives of comrades. It was not uncommon for a soldier on leave to sacrifice some of his precious time to visit the parents of a friend at the front – a gesture of true comradeship. Neither could the authorities shield the home population from the necessity of informing next-of-kin of the deaths of their sons and relatives. More than one in ten soldiers were killed, so that there was hardly a family who was not directly bereaved or knew someone who was. The propaganda must have been seriously weakened by the dawning realisation that all was not so rosy as was claimed in the press.

That pre-war society was still class-ridden is amply evidenced by the simple fact that officers could write what they wished. No doubt they had strict codes of honour not to prejudice the morale of the recipients of their letters, but in any case parents and wives of 'officers and gentlemen' would be thought incapable of passing on any negative comments about the war to the lower classes, who, in their ignorance, might somehow be damaged by bad news.

For the divisions and brigades, censorship was probably a full-time job, perhaps for an older officer, or one who had been wounded. For smaller units the officer in charge performed the duties as censor of the letters of his own men.

Almost all of Willie's letters were in the official envelopes, all-over green in colour and later buff with green stripes. A few were in ordinary stamped envelopes, some posted in Britain, having been 'smuggled' there by friends, and, very rarely, field postcards. Occasionally he apologised to his parents for a delay in writing because he did not have a 'green':

I have, as you know, up to now used only green envelopes for my communications to you. The ordinary envelopes, which must be censored, compel one to be more or less stiff in his correspondence. Consequently, having been able to pick up a few 'greens' over and above the issue, which is only one a week, I have been able to use them for some time. However, having run short, I have delayed my letter, expecting every day to get a green envelope. I got one today, hence this scribble. [6/2/16]

Sometimes too, a 'green' could be acquired from a friend or even shared in the following way:

If I am not writing quite so often as before it is because we are in a quiet place and consequently fairly safe and news is scarce. Green envelopes are also scarce and on this occasion, being without one myself, my friend Bradley has graciously suggested that I send my letter in his envelope for his parents to post to you, hence the Blighty postmark (Blackburn) which ought to be on the envelope. When I get a 'green un' I shall probably do the same for Bradley. [7/1/16]

Just how sensitive the censorship was is demonstrated by an apparently innocuous remark, which was passed, but only after reference to the illness of a comrade had been lightly scored out but not obliterated:

All my chums in the section are as well as yours truly Chisnall has gone 'down the line' with scabies. This is the second departure from the section. More than anyone else, even to a ridiculous pitch, Chisnall has always been keen on personal cleanliness and yet he has contracted scabies. We are all sorry for him. [28/3/17]

Willie often mentioned his frustration at being restricted by the rules:

I can assure you that it is very difficult to concoct a decent sized letter from the material at hand considering that one is forbidden to mention the names of places or military detail. [9/1/16]

I am quite well and on the whole enjoying my work here. I must not tell you how far from the fighting area we are or give any clue as to my whereabouts except that we are somewhere in France. If I did mention where I was the letter, in all probability, would be destroyed. Perhaps I am allowed to say that I am not in the battle area yet. [11/9/15]

It was with pleasure that I read in your letter that on no occasion has any of mine been mutilated by the censor. I do not think you can realise how difficult it is to write an interesting letter. If they are one scrap interesting it is something accomplished, for the difficulty of writing, when one cannot really mention the war, is very hard. [18/12/15]

The letters were of course almost invariably interesting, but some of the less imaginative men had real difficulty when they were not allowed to write about the war:

The great trouble is that the most popular subject, the war, is forbidden. I have seen one or two of the boys sit with open pad and poised pencil for an hour or so trying to think of something to write and in despair, when darkness begins to fall, rapidly scribbling a field card and, giving vent to a contented sigh, drop it in the post box. [8/8/18]

Even though many letters were not censored, the process was something of a lottery and the risk of being hauled before the censor and severely punished was far too great for the writer to take too many liberties. The punishment for transgressing the rules could be quite extreme:

Your suggestion that one of my civilian friends should send you a few lines in French has been on my mind for some time but in view of recent orders and warnings that we have received I deem it imprudent to encourage this. Quite unintentionally 'Monsieur' may put in his letter (if it were to be written) something of a military nature and then we should have trouble. One section of the orders which we have recently had sets out the case of a Canadian soldier who had arranged for a civilian to send a letter home stating his whereabouts. The thing was discovered and the soldier has been sentenced to twelve months' hard labour so you will understand that I prefer to leave the matter alone. [22/1/17]

Willie did try to circumvent the censor in his early days by using a code. This consisted of putting a dot above certain letters in the narrative to spell out, over several sentences, the desired message. He used this to tell his parents where he was in his early days in the war zone so that for example in September 1915 he was able to convey '*I have been near the trenches by Maben*'. He soon dropped this practice, however, no doubt because of the risk involved. Another device to get round the location issue was devised by Tom Whittaker, who was shrewd enough to work out where his son might be from general content of the letters and the aid of a map of northern France. Inward mail was not censored and Tom evidently suggested a possible location. In his reply Willie wrote:

The village in which we are now is very clean and quiet and fortunately big enough to contain one or two decent cafes. Which reminds me that your surmise is quite correct. [18/9/16]

Sometimes a hint about military operations was risked and the following remark, clearly indicating a military build up, evidently went unchallenged:

I could fill half a dozen pages with nothing but war items but – after arousing your curiosity by the above few words I will attempt to satisfy it. THERE IS SOMETHING GOING ON. [3/7/16]

The Battle of the Somme started four days later!

The censor for Willie's section was, until March 1917, their own officer, Captain W. D. Carruthers. This officer would sign with his rank and name at the bottom of some of the letters.

Willie noted the departure of Carruthers with regret and even some bitterness:

Our late officer, Captain Carruthers appears to have left us for good now and our new CO is Captain McPherson. Since his arrival we have been delayed with orders and we shall —, but I forgot, one must not say all one would like and anyway the war will soon be over. [21/3/17]

One can only speculate what the mysterious blank above referred to, but in subsequent correspondence it was clear that the new man was not popular in that he had made the men work harder and was a poor communicator.

Censorship did catch up with Willie in a way which could have had very serious consequences for him. He often philosophised about the war and in one letter recounted a dream which he attributed to an infantryman he had met and which centred on the futility and pointlessness of war. In the dream the two sides fraternised to the extent that all the men decided that it was not a good idea to continue fighting and declared peace. This letter never reached home as it was destroyed by the censor. Undeterred, however, Willie then recounted the following version of the dream in his next letter, minus the description of the reaction of the troops, which was evidently the aspect that had broken all the rules:

Speaking about the infantry reminded me of a fantastical dream that was related to me by an infantry acquaintance.

He commenced the story by carrying my memory back to last Christmas day, when you will remember that the Hun and Tommy joined together in no-man's-land to share smokes and drinks together and to sing Christmas hymns. Now for the dream:

On Christmas day this year history repeated itself and friend and foe met and fraternised between the trenches, but with a great difference, for instead of being confined to one little area the spirit animated every soldier on all the fronts. Now, when the soldiers were making merry, the thoughtful ones (who are well represented in the army today) began to realise how wonderful this break in the hostilities was and after a little debating they threw down their rifles with cries of 'To hell with war and death'. In the dream the cry was carried from mouth to mouth and in a few hours fighting was a thing of the past.

Or course, the point of the story is 'Peace on earth and goodwill to all men.' [9/12/16]

The first letter was read by the censor and Willie was hauled before him. He was told that this kind of defeatist thinking was the worst kind of offence in its potential to damage civilian morale, and if it had not been for his obvious intelligence and contrition he would have been punished. This would have meant a blot on his record, which could have had serious consequences when he came to look for a job after the war. Willie apologised and said that the letter had been written in ignorance and requested humbly that the letter be destroyed:

I have been waiting until I got a green envelope to tell you of an incident which occurred in connection with the letter I wrote a few days ago. I refer to the one in which I related the 'dream' I had heard from an infantry acquaintance. The original letter told the story of the dream and ended with a few lines about the feelings of the troops. I obviously cannot repeat these lines as this letter may also be censored. At any rate, the upshot was that the officer who censored the letter had me before him and gave me a long lecture about its contents. He said that had he not recognised from the letter that he had to deal with an educated man I should have been 'crimed'. The fact is that I had allowed a little pessimism to creep into the words and, although the officer confessed that my statements were no doubt true, he said that my words were calculated to cause a feeling of unrest in Britain.

I was told that I had committed the most serious offence possible in letter writing. However after sincere apologies and a confession that I had a fit of the dumps when I wrote the letter I suggested to the officer that he burn the letter. He did this and then I came back to the billet and wrote the letter which you actually received. [19/12/16]

Willie was genuinely surprised that his innocent narrative of the dream, which he confessed in a later letter had been a complete invention on his part, had caused such a reaction and he evidently received wise advice from home about his future conduct:

I realise, with you, that one must not defy the censor and no one was more surprised than me to be 'pulled over the coals'.

However, I intend to trouble him no more for my greatest wish is to leave the army with a clean sheet. [1/1/17]

Captain Carruthers, who was presumably the censoring officer, was a member of the upper classes and was described by Willie as a 'varsity man'. He was pleased that someone in this category had praised his intellectual ability. He seems to have held his CO in awe.

There was no way a lad of humble origin from a Northern industrial town could ever aspire to going to university or of becoming an officer, however well qualified. The change in social attitudes by the start of the Second World War, just over twenty years later, is described later but is perhaps dramatically emphasised by the fact that William Whittaker was appointed commanding officer of the 33rd Home Guard Battalion of the Duke of Wellington's Regiment in 1940 with the rank of Major – one level senior to Captain Carruthers!

6

War

The censorship rules made it impossible for the troops to write with complete frankness about the war, but they could still convey some idea of what was going on. The initial mood of euphoria engendered by the belief that the war would be of short duration gradually evaporated, leading to a rather more pessimistic tone, but this and general remarks about the progress of the conflict seem not to have been forbidden. In any case these were often influenced by the content of communiqués to the troops from high-ranking officers, which were in effect propaganda, so that any general comments in letters home were likely to reinforce the official line. It was also possible to share philosophical thoughts about warfare.

There is no doubt that details of the worst horrors were not disclosed to the men, who had to rely on their own observations, word of mouth, the limited amount of sanitised information handed down from above and articles in the British press. Many of the men had newspapers sent from home and sometimes they were able to buy them:

I manage to get a newspaper almost every day – they cost twopence a copy and find that we are daily raiding and strafing

Fritz on some part of the front or other. The raids seem to be very successful and must be having a demoralising effect on the foe. [22/1/17]

I read the speech by Sir Douglas Haig a few days ago and it certainly indicated a very firm state of mind. The news seems to be very good throughout. I am sure that we all hope that his prognostications will be correct and that 1917 will be the peace year. The general opinion most certainly favours an early end to this most dreadful war. [19/2/17]

This kind of propaganda fed to the troops suggested that the allies were winning the war when in reality it was stalemate:

My whole being is permeated with joy at the recent successes. It must be wonderful news to you but imagine what it feels like to us out here. All these victories strengthen our hopes of an early finish. I can truthfully say that there is a more contented look on every face and there is a more optimistic vein in every conversation. Two hundred villages retaken. It is wonderful and I almost feel like singing and dancing. Although I prophesy the continuation of these advances I also realise that we are many miles from Germany. I move about daily in areas where one dare not show his head above ground and conditions like these are obviously not conducive to hilarity. [21/3/17]

There was a more realistic tone about the extent of the ground gained in the following extract:

The war news of late is more cheering. The successes in the Messines front line are very satisfactory and Fritz must feel shaky because of these lightning and unexpected assaults. Although on the face of it, our gains seem to be very small, I and anyone else who has been in the country around the Messines district know them to be very important. [10/6/17]

That the communiqués from High Command were carefully worded in order to raise morale is amply illustrated by the information passed down after some of the bloodiest battles. They must have been woefully short on detail and with the hindsight of knowledge we could hardly describe these hideous events as glorious successes when hundreds of thousands of lives had been sacrificed for virtually no ground gained, and with losses, dead and wounded, often higher than those suffered by the Germans in the same incidents:

We have been enduring some fine weather but now the sun is doing his bit right well for October. My heartfelt hope is that the sun will continue to bestow his warmth upon us for it is by his help alone that we can continue the glorious successes achieved round Ypres. I should perhaps say around Passchendaele, Hollebeke and Broodseinde. [14/10/17]

In spite of not being aware of the vast scale of casualties in those battles, where there were some 250,000 British casualties, Willie experienced plenty of death and destruction at first hand involving troops on both sides. Shortly after his arrival at the front, and still a boy of eighteen, he wrote:

It was a remarkable thing at Vermelles to see the new regiments going in for their first taste. They were all glum and depressed at the thought of what the next few hours would bring forth and their faces were strained and grim. This was not actually with fear but chiefly, I think, with doggedness. Then on the same day, a few hours afterwards to see the remains of the regiments who had been many times in the thick of it. They laughed and sang and joked and threw kisses to the French girls and to put it bluntly didn't care a damn. These fellows, who must before the war have valued their lives above all else now go, without thought, to risk their lives with smiling faces. It is a paradox. [17/10/15]

We saw German prisoners, straight from the trenches, being marched into Bethune. There were two or three hundred of them. They were muddy, bloody and with characteristic German faces. They were the most pitiable, dejected and sorry crowd I have ever set eyes upon. Here was one with a face covered in blood from his own wounds, here another with a bloodstained bandage on his bullet head and here and there others who limped painfully along because of their wounded legs or bodies. To make even worse this miserable sight, the rain was pouring in torrents and many of the prisoners were without head covering and some were minus jackets. These men would, I am sure, be pitied in England but here there is no pity. This war is too real and to us the atrocities of the Germans, possibly of some of these very prisoners are also too real. Because of this, the prisoners are jibed and hooted and ridiculed. Had the local inhabitants had weapons I would not have given a snap of the finger for the lives of these men.

On another occasion, when a solitary couple of prisoners were being escorted down the road past our billet they were knocked down by two or three hefty 'Jocks'. Had not an important officer intervened these soldiers would have been killed and I, who saw the whole incident, would at that moment have enjoyed seeing those men done in. Such is the effect of war. Of course, that mood happily passed away and I feel surprised that it was ever present. Every horror was near at that period and for a time it turned one's mind but now we are accustomed to it and treat such affairs with 'sang froid'. [18/12/15]

So much have times changed that in a twenty-first century war those 'Jocks' would have faced a trial and the possibility of long prison sentences.

I was most excited when first entering the battle zone and had the most strange tight feeling in my innards. We arrived at night. We had no idea how far we were from the Germans and did not know whether the loud explosions were of our own shells or theirs bursting two miles away though it seemed like only a few hundred yards that first night. Star shells were flaring, shells were bursting with little flashes and through it all could be heard the continuous rattle of rifle fire. In addition to all these strange sights and sounds, the wounded men were passing in one long line of ambulances. The noise was unbearable and we were told that because of the shortage of Red Cross men we should, in a few minutes, have to go into the trenches. Imagine our feelings! Fortunately we were not called upon although there is no doubt it was a near thing. [1/1/16]

I saw a rather sad and pathetic sight the other day. I was talking to a sanitary Corporal of a certain regiment when I observed in the distance, at the end of the street, soldiers coming along wheeling something, a bundle wrapped in green canvas – a dead body. The striking thing was that every Tommy all along the road sprang to attention and saluted as the corpse passed by. I saw no exception and the command of an officer was unnecessary. [17/1/17]

Willie often saw dead and wounded men but was only rarely able to write about it. He must have been risking the censor's wrath even to pen the following:

There are horrible sights around here. It is common to see decaying limbs protruding from the ground and from the sides of trenches and so on. On first sight one shudders and feels sick. On second sight one considers and observes the gruesome scene from a sanitary point of view and gradually walks by without thinking of them. They are taken as a matter of course. [17/8/17]

Destruction and the debris of war were commonplace:

This place is a great disordered wilderness of torn and gaping barbed wire, of battered trenches, shell torn ground, great big mine craters, untold rubbish and withal an indescribable smell. [25/8/16]

The Battle of the Somme was only weeks away when Willie was able to describe the great contrast between the idyllic scenes of peace and the grim reality of war and to anticipate the major event which he was aware was about to happen and which he referred to as 'The great advance':

I am writing this letter in a little hut adjoining the water tanks where I am on duty. Stretching from my hut for about a mile there are flat, wonderfully cultivated, fields which exhibit the charm and spirit of Spring. The colours are fresh and green and the regularity is only broken here and there where a red roofed farmhouse stands or where a few cattle are grazing. Beyond the fields lies Mont X, one of the highest points for many a mile around and its sides are covered with a great forest of beautiful trees. From my hut the view is full of peace and life and beyond, an occasional lorry or wagon passes along the white road in the middle distance. There is nothing to remind you of the war. Peace and life here and only two miles away war and death. Thick fields of wheat, corn and barley here, black, bare, cheerless ground where shells and bullets fly there.

One must not compare unless he desires to be miserable, so let us say hurrah for the fine weather, our boys are not now up to the waist in icy cold water. Let us say hurrah for conscription, more men can come to France. The more men there are here the easier it will be for those already here.

Their lot will not be so hard when the great advance does commence. Our soldiers will fight all the better and braver knowing that reinforcements will be to hand. Support failed to turn up at Loos and the advance was less than it could and should have been. But in the great battle which still has to be fought the support will be there, thousands of them to fill the gaps immediately and the advance will be all the more than we expected.

I read Sir Douglas Haig's report which says how well our boys are carrying on, our air service is wonderful, our soldiers are brave and cheerful, our medical services are magnificent. Reading between the lines everything is A one and O.K. [31/5/17]

This last passage shows just how the troops accepted the bland words of the Commander in Chief, which to the reader of today are clearly designed only with morale in mind and completely omitting any mention of the reality of static trench-bound warfare.

The Somme was specifically noted because a film of the battle had been made, no doubt for propaganda purposes. Talking movies were not to be invented for another decade so the film was silent. It was shown in Blighty as well as France:

The incidents in the Battle of the Somme picture which you describe are very familiar. Although the sights are horrible enough you are fortunately spared the sounds of the battle. The terrible whistle of an approaching shell raises one's hair and is only eclipsed by the rattle of a descending bomb in all its awfulness. Then there are the horrible sounds of the Dressing Posts and the great roar of the artillery. You are fortunately spared all this. [11/9/16]

Far from resenting the censorship, although it was obviously inconvenient at times, the troops evidently felt that they themselves had a duty to protect those at home from some of the worst news:

I saw the Somme film the other day. I do not know whether we saw an uncensored edition or not but the opinion of most present was that there are several parts which should not be shown in England. Very strong opinions were expressed upon the point. You will easily understand that the picture generally was a dull sort of affair to all of us for most of the scenes depicted we see almost every day. We recognised many of the views and are all agreed that it is a marvellous piece of photography. [22/1/17]

The futility of the most infamous battle of the war was evidently covered up by the authorities and the gain of a few hundred yards of mud and a row of enemy trenches was presented as a victory in the film.

Willie visited trenches captured from the Germans and after commenting on perceived success made the following observations about the better construction of the enemy defences:

All the news of late is wonderfully cheering but the advances are accomplished at what cost. If you had walked into the trenches

*and dugouts which the Germans occupied a few months ago
you would more than ever realise what a cunning fox the
enemy is. Deep and well made they afford more protection
than our own and this fact makes our present advances all the
more remarkable. [1/9/16]*

The new secret weapon, the tank, had been through its early
paces on the Somme front, and when Willie was moved away
from that area, one of his greatest regrets was expressed:

*We are in a part now which seems all the more quiet because
we have been down THERE. We are spared the sound from
many hundreds of guns and we are able to retire at night
certain of at least a few hours sleep. I am rather sorry that we
left the other place without seeing the tanks. They seem to be
wonderful monsters and I think that their use will save many
men's lives. One of our wags says that they will shorten the
war by five years – cheerful! [27/9/16]*

The section was soon back in the line however – possibly its
temporary detachment from the Somme area was planned to
give them some physical relief from the incessant noise and
stress of the conflict:

*Now that I am on duty so near the line I have had many
exciting times. My head rings continually with the noise from
the guns and I am quite near them all day long. The shrapnel
helmet also gives one a headache and I feel relieved each night
when I can doff it and wear my ordinary hat. [23/11/16]*

The helmets, or tin hats as they were known, could be quite debilitating if worn for any length of time. There were quieter periods, however:

You must not worry about my proximity to the line. It is exceptionally quiet and on the days I have been up to the front line trenches I have had no cause to worry. [3/2/16]

Service in or near the line was of course a normal requirement, and Willie was unselfishly generous in his thoughts about the recipient of the next leave warrant:

When the first leave warrant comes in I think Black will be the lucky recipient. He certainly deserves it having done nearly three months up the line continuously. He is still up there while I am still at Headquarters. Mellor, a reinforcement, who is doing his first turn up there has been very ill and queer. Mellor asked to come away and I expected to go up to replace him but the officer was adamant and made Mellor carry on there, saying that he must become accustomed to the dangerous district as other men had to. [3/6/17]

There was scant room for compassion as it would be all too easy for less-committed men to say 'I don't feel well' or 'I don't like it here' or 'I am too old' in the expectation of someone else having to replace them in a dangerous location. Shell shock was becoming recognised as a genuine problem, but malingering could not be tolerated and the officers had little alternative but to take a firm line. The tragic case and sympathetic treatment of one member of the section, Sambo Mills, is recounted later, but one old veteran, a regular soldier who was seconded to the section to recuperate, got no such concession:

I am sorry to say that Joe Archer, one of the attached men, has had to return to his unit in the 24th Division for he was a jolly comrade and had been with us for seven months. He is about forty three years old and it seems very hard that he had to return to a fighting unit. [3/6/17]

The soldiers were evidently aware of some of the wider issues of the war, probably gleaned from British newspapers. It is rather surprising to note that news of a German victory was sometimes reported:

What do you think of the Rumanian rout? It is astonishing that she should be so unprepared and particularly after two years of observing Germany's fighting methods. Horatio Bottomley's parrot-like phrase seems very apt – somebody blundered. I can assure you that I hold no brief for Deutchland but on looking the facts in the face it is obvious to me that Germany is winning. She is fighting in any country but her own, she is swamping Rumania and she still keeps a pretty good line on the Somme. I am no pessimist and I know that we shall win in the end but I am afraid the war will last a long time yet. [3/12/16]

Within three weeks the mood had swung completely the other way:

The peace offers from Germany and the formation of a determined government have bucked everybody out here wonderfully. I meet few who do not expect to be in civvies by this time next Christmas. A very popular feeling is that we shall have peace before next Autumn. [16/12/16]

Willie was nevertheless well aware that Britain continued not to have all its own way:

The news is still good, with the exception of the U-boat work, which from Fritz's point of view must be very satisfactory. Sixty four ships sunk in a week. [24/4/17]

The success of the U-boat campaign, starving Britain of American aid, led to the most disastrous decision by the German High Command, to authorise attacks on American shipping. This undoubtedly swung public opinion in the USA and made it politically possible to send American troops to Europe in 1918. Willie was on the one hand elated by the arrival of the Yankees, but still recognised the German threat as they threw everything into one last desperate attempt to break the allies:

We are safe and sound, though just a little worried at the success of Fritz. I am confident that the enemy will be brought to a standstill but it is galling to have to admit that the hun has retaken almost all the ground we so dearly bought in 1916. When his advance is stopped, as it most surely will be, he will have gained a little but lost out of all proportion to his gains. The very fact of his breaking our line constitutes a failure and must demoralise his troops enormously. Ironbound by discipline they have been massed to attack, realising that their lives have not been taken into account. It seems to me that he will never recover numerical superiority for as month follows month, with America's aid, our numbers enlarge and Germany's decrease. It is my opinion that this attack is the last feverish effort of our enemy to beat us before America can give us her complete assistance and if it fails he is beaten more surely than ever before. [1/4/18]

The Germans were driven to this last push by the success of the Allies' own blockade on Germany, where there were strikes by civilians and protests about the deterioration in living conditions. On the British side there were desperate calls for reinforcements to make good losses in the line and to halt the German advance. Willie did not disclose to his parents something which he told his own family years later. It was contemplated that some RAMC men would be sent up the line as infantrymen and out of his section Willie's name was the only one on the list. He was sure he had been singled out by a vindictive staff sergeant at the section headquarters because of some imagined impertinence.

The British Expeditionary Force was in France and Belgium to hold that part of the front and hopefully advance towards Germany. The only other help they had was from a small number of Canadians. The French troops were engaged further south and for the most part of the war, the British hardly saw French soldiers, who were known as 'poilus', let alone other nationalities. The arrival of the Americans, Portuguese and many colonials changed all that as the conflict neared its end:

How cosmopolitan is northern France in these troubled times. Looking out from the window of an estaminet in the main square of a small nearby town I saw in less than ten minutes, Englishmen, Canadians, Australians, Americans, Zouaves, Chinese, Portuguese, French and Belgians. The common language between most of them is French. Even the Chinese, with their flat faces and narrow eyes can usually say 'bonjour' and 'Allemagne non bon'. You should hear the Yanks talking broken French with their atrocious nasal twang. One came into the estaminet the other night and asked for 'blink blank' – I suppose he meant vin blanc. After trying about four times and succeeding not he turned from the bar and, somewhat disgruntled, said 'Say boys this yer woman don't understand her own goddamned lingo' I translated the order and both the Yank and the lady smiled their thanks. [2/8/18]

The war dragged on but the news, propaganda or not, was more cheering:

Hasn't the recent news been stimulating? The capitulation of Bulgaria opens up possibilities of a much earlier peace, especially when one considers the unenviable position Turkey now holds. Possibly when you receive this letter the Turk will have retired not only from in front of Allenby's army but from the war altogether. If Turkey drops out the consummation of the war before Christmas becomes a possibility. However, one cannot tell what will happen if the army in front of us begins to advance rapidly again. Within the limits imposed by the censor I will try to tell you all the news as quickly as possible. [5/10/18]

Just one month later news of victory was in the air:

Here we are again, still smiling in the face of discomfort and more broadly at the continued good news. How many more weeks? is the cry. Laughter and jokes at the downfall of the Germans are rife and those of us who have crossed over the newly liberated territory realise how completely Jerry has been beaten. It is evident from the fresh untouched areas where the farmers are doing their winter work on the land, through the desolate devastated districts where the war has raged for four years and where every scene speaks sadly of the hell which Tommy has braved to bring the world to these happy days which are now in sight. The freed civilians cannot do enough in their appreciation of Britain's doggedness and success. Tout est bien.

It is hard to realise that only a few short weeks ago German soldiers were walking about in the very streets where at this precise moment a group of lads are singing, very appropriately, 'The great big world keeps turning'. In daytime, Fritz's recent occupation is apparent but happily all traces of it are being deleted as quickly as possible. For instance take the streets. Each of these our enemy had renamed in bold white lettering using his own ugly language. He had written Kaiser Strasse and Kirche Strasse and Tirpitz Platz in three foot letters on any wall, board or suitable object which took his bullying fancy and in their place, in characteristically English style we have Rue de Roi. Rue L'eglise and Place Jerome. [5/11/18]

The Armistice, which amounted to unconditional surrender by the Germans, was signed six days later on 11 November 1918:

The news of the armistice was received here in a quiet manner except for a general feeling of relief, which had expression in every face and voice. There was no display of rowdyism. Everybody seemed dazed by the news. [8/12/18]

With an air of anti-climax, therefore, the war came to an end!

/

Shelling

Shelling was employed in two ways. Artillery was used to prepare the way for any planned advance by an intense barrage of shellfire aimed first at the enemy lines then, when it was time for the men to go over the top, the range would be extended so that the shells passed over the heads of the British troops and continued to pound German positions a little further forward. The second use was more of a psychological nature, to soften up the opposition with fear and noise. Of course, this was a reciprocal practice with fire in both directions deafening and frightening both sets of combatants.

The countless missiles, though deadly, actually claimed fewer lives than the rifle and machine-gun fire that dominated the major battles, but shelling was regarded so importantly that the British High Command was calling for more ammunition rather than more men before the Battle of the Somme, the start of which had to be postponed until more supplies had arrived.

The shells themselves were made in munitions factories, with the cases being hand filled, mostly by female labour. The skin of these workers gradually turned yellow, and no doubt powder was inhaled, causing potential long-term health problems. There were scant health-and-safety regulations in those days. Manufacturing techniques must have been fairly primitive as many shells, both German and British, failed to explode. Readers of the famous German war novel *All Quiet on the Western Front* will be well aware of the high failure rate of British missiles.

Shells did cause many deaths and injuries, but the main tangible effects were that whole villages were razed to the ground, woodland was reduced to stumps and no man's land to a sea of mud. Even today, when visiting battlegrounds where museums have been established, one can see areas of ground still pitted with shell craters. Paradoxically, some of these craters actually saved lives, as some men, wounded in the fighting, crawled into them for shelter.

Although never subject to the hail of bullets endured by the infantry, the RAMC boys were frequently exposed to enemy shellfire and bombing raids.

The side effects of the shelling were also significant, such as the reaction of the pack animals and the plight of the civilians whose homes were devastated and their whole village reduced to rubble:

Last night they sent half a dozen shells over at about half past nine. The horses that were tethered in the village were brought along past our tent by fellows, most of whom had just fallen asleep before the trouble started. The horses were taken into a field close to the frontier until the danger was considered to be over. [18/7/16]

It is a touching sight to see the half-demented villagers running away from their houses, some of them half dressed with slippers on and some of the youngsters in their shirts or nightdresses only and with bare feet. There are two roads leading to safety from this village and these are thick with the poor civilians. Here you see the nuns who are bravely trying to run a school for the children so that their education shall not be imperilled by the war. The nuns are running along the road and at every report, whether of our own or the German guns, throw themselves down in the road. It is scenes like this that make one thankful that it is not being carried out in Blighty. I wonder if these young kiddies will remember the awful happenings. I hope not, for if they do their nerves will suffer. [18/7/16]

For the most part, however, shelling was regarded by Tommy as a fact of life and Willie was often able to take a somewhat nonchalant approach, no doubt partly to reassure his parents:

We have had the deuce of a day. Fritz has been shelling heavily all around us but good luck still favours us. At this moment the shells are dropping about a hundred and fifty yards away. Of course, we are used to this kind of thing and are worried very little. [8/1/16]

It is terrible to think of the men in the trenches on a night like this. It is very wild and the guns are blazing away at their hardest. Our little hut shakes at the force of the explosions.

They fire all night but I can honestly say they have never affected my night's rest. [11/1/16]

The next morning he heard that two of his comrades, Woolfe and Cannon, had been under particularly heavy shellfire and had been lucky not to be hit. Eventually he had to admit to sleepless nights, caused by the shelling but also by the insect life:

Fortunately the mosquitoes, those other and more dangerous tormentors of mankind, have not affected us except to prevent our sleep. We are having the devil's luck. At times the noise of the guns is so loud that no individual explosion can be heard and one feels as if his brain would snap and he would go mad. We are chattering with one another and smoking all night long. It would be unbearable if one was alone. [4/8/16]

Several incidents were recounted which were by no means to be shrugged off as inconsequential:

Now that I am so near the line I am thankful that the Germans are quieter than they might be. My head rings continually with the noise of the guns and I am quite near them all day long. [23/11/16]

The other day I had a very good jaunt on the lorry. Along with Black I went to draw some materials for building incinerators from the dump. We then had to deliver them to a place perhaps a mile from the Germans. We were well out of sight however, being on the other side of the hill from the trenches. We went through Armentiers where the roads are screened and where one sees, at various intervals, cheerful notices such as 'Do not loiter, this place is liable to be shelled' or 'This road is subject to very heavy shellfire' and so on. Going through X we passed the communications trenches around hell fire corner which are named after London streets on our way to Y. This journey took me nearer to the trenches than I have been so far but fortunately things were very quiet and we had no excitement. Returning safely, I was not sorry we had had the trip. [4/5/16]

On his many spells of duty in the trenches, Willie was often directly affected by shellfire:

The news still seems to be good. America is backing us and internally Germany seems to be shaky. I have also reason to believe that the German army is also shaky. It is getting shelled enough at any rate and not without reciprocation, for Corporal Black, Marfleet and I, on the little sub-section, have been shelled out of our billet and are now living together in a cellar. We have a decent fire and beds of a sort and are reasonably comfortable. [4/4/17]

Then to B-G where we had more thrills than I cared for. Having two billets struck by shells we found refuge in a cellar and came out unscathed. [1/9/17]

Later in the war he recounted one really lucky escape in his usual enthralling prose:

I think I had my narrowest squeak of my whole time in France. Coming back from duty at dinnertime, with Salter, we noticed new shell holes and damage as we approached our dugout. We had been away for about three hours and had no idea at what time of the morning the shelling had occurred. At the dugout we met Marfleet and Williamson who were also as ignorant. Salter hung out his washing. We then followed the other two for about twenty yards over the uneven ground to get our dinner. We were going across open ground when the fearful devilish whistle of two big shells coming right at us was heard. Throwing plate, mug, knife and fork anywhere we dropped flat and hugged the earth with an intensity you could not imagine – all hope gone – dead for certain: crash! bang! still alive! We were lifted, without exaggeration, six inches from the ground by the concussion, smothered with loose earth, stones and so on. Then we were running with bent body to cover before the next should come: crash! bang! Not so near this time. Another sprint then another and so on from cover to cover for about three hundred yards until we reached the cookhouse. We had dinner, Salter and I, and after about half an hour the storm ceased and we returned, in fear and trembling, all the way to our dugout. Salter's washing was riddled with holes. Our dugout door was splintered and broken. One shell had landed about five yards from the door. Where were Marfleet and Williamson? We were standing at the door when some fellows passed and on enquiry they told us that at least one fellow had copped out. He had a plate and mug in his hand and was lying a short distance away next to an old German gun carriage. An awful fear struck us. Was it

*one of our comrades? Salter and I went to see and we would
have been unable to tell who it was except that it was not one
of our boys as the poor fellow wore no red cross. Williamson
and Marfleet turned up about an hour later. They had been
in their dugout all the time. I was slightly wounded as a small
shell fragment gave me a cut on the hand. [22/1/18]*

Other colleagues were also just as lucky:

*Our Staff Sergeant has just been in to pay us our money. He
has been up to pay the other boys who are nearer the line
and who have had a very narrow escape. He was standing in
the middle of the road, having just got out of the car, when a
piece of shell fell within a foot of him. He has got the piece
as a souvenir. [6/2/16]*

*Corporal Black and Cannon are having it pretty hot in their
area of duty. Cannon relieved me and from accounts I have
been spared some nerve-racking experiences. I had had enough
before I was relieved. Black and Cannon have had their billet
blown up twice in two days and consequently have had three
different billets in as many days. They were fortunately out
on both occasions. As I have told you before we have got the
devil's luck in this section. [8/5/17]*

*Black was wounded by a piece of shell about a week ago. An
officer had already been struck and whilst Black was bandaging
him another shell landed about twenty yards away and a piece
struck him just below the right breast pocket and came out at*

*the side of his tunic doing little more than a graze to the skin.
It was a narrow escape. He is quite well and back on duty but
I think his nerves are a bit shaky. [27/6/16]*

Corporal Black was evidently suffering from delayed shock.
As mentioned earlier, the condition which was to become
known as shell shock was only gradually being recognised
and there was a difficult line to be drawn between genuine
cases and malingerers who might lay claim to this condition
as a means of getting out of the fighting. From the incidents
described above it is clear that virtually any soldier could
make some sort of a case of having been affected mentally
by the shelling. Most just got on with the job even though,
like Willie, they had had enough, or like Black, they had
shaky nerves. Men suspected of trying it on were given
short shrift and put back into their units with a caution, but
more serious cases could be court-martialled for cowardice.
There are several reported cases of men who may well have
been suffering from severe shell shock, having refused to go
over the top into battle, being executed by firing squad to
encourage the others.

One member of the 41st Section did become a victim of
shock and his condition was recognised:

*Mills has had a nervous breakdown owing to the dangerous
locality where he and Corporal Lanigan have been very much
shelled. I have not seen Mills but I believe that he looks very bad
and it is said that he may go home to England to recuperate.
Four members of the section we relieved and whose billets we*

now occupy also broke down when in this location and one of them, I believe, is properly off his head. This district is classed as extremely dangerous and men billeted here dare not venture out from the billets in groups. There is a German observation balloon from which every movement in the town can be seen and if a few men are observed together they form a good mark as the shells then land dangerously near. I feel sorry for Mills. I do not think anyone will take his place. [15/1/16]

The authorities abandoned that extremely dangerous district, which brings into question why men were sent there in the first place. There are many examples in the letters of this kind of thoughtlessness and lack of concern for the well-being of the troops. Poor Mills would be sent back to a nursing home in England, several having been set up specifically for genuine shell shock victims, many of whom were to suffer permanent brain damage.

Willie marched into a village where there had been death as well as destruction:

At the right incline, about three miles away, was hill 60. As we approached the village of X we could see how strenuously it had been shelled. The road was cut up by shells and on each side the trees had, in many cases, been burnt and torn by the shells. Here and there by the roadside were huge shell holes full of water in which, without exaggeration, two huge motor lorries could easily be accommodated. The first street we entered in this ruined town is absolutely razed to the ground. The highest piece of wall standing was no more than four feet from the ground. All around was debris and in the cellars which were not too choked up one could see mattresses floating in the water. Also littered about there were bedsteads, cupboards and chairs – grim relics indeed. Here and there, where there was a patch of ground of any size were little white crosses on mounds of earth; English soldiers' graves. Feeling that no ruin, however bad, would affect me. I was surprised when I saw the remains of the once fine church. Although I pride myself on being able to control my feelings fairly well, I almost cried. The tall steeple was completely destroyed, the debris was twenty feet high and more in some places. The stained glass windows are shattered and all the woodwork is burnt away. The effect of all this destruction is very depressing and how it makes one hate the Germans. [21/1/16]

New Year's Eve 1916 brought a momentary cessation in the constant barrage as both sides paused for a few hours to bring in the new year. Willie was right in the battle zone observing the scene:

Ring out the old, ring in the new. As you see I am writing this on new year's day. Had I been in England I should maybe have had a holiday instead of which I have been 'camping out'. I was up the line and from my point of vantage, about three or four hundred yards from the trenches I gazed upon no-man's-land. The ground that stretched before me was ploughed and disfigured with numerous shells and shell holes. From my peephole the view was very comprehensive. Ahead were villages and towns held by Fritz and I could trace most of his communication trenches on the way up to his front line and in all this area I saw no soul. All seemed dead or asleep. Here and there I observed a little patch of grass which was much more noticeable because of its isolation. These little patches are daring attempts of mother nature to raise her head in unnatural surroundings.

The guns were quiet and during my brief survey there was not even a rifle shot to disturb the deathly stillness. The quiet was intense. I even spoke to my comrades in a whisper. Shush, nothing moved, even the wind was quiet. Then, Crack! The quietness was broken and as if the solitary rifle shot was a signal the guns opened up – boom boom. From my nest I saw the shells drop. I saw the earth and smoke rush into the air and then I heard the dull crash – business as usual; the brief period of stillness was over and may not occur again for weeks or months. Crash! Bang! Take that and that! And I murmur with pleasure at the efforts of our artillery. 'Give it 'em hot, let 'em have it. Every shell we fire is putting fear into the enemy's heart.' He replies very feebly. 'I wonder if the censor would be very annoyed if I expressed an opinion that the Germans have not got enough shells to give us tit for tat.' [1/1/17]

The devastation caused by shelling was graphically described after the Battle of the Somme, which reduced some whole towns and villages to heaps of rubble:

We returned to Albert where the statue of The Lady of the Lamp, holding a baby, hangs in a striking position over the busy street. How horribly ruined was Albert. The crumbling houses, the street strewn and even blocked with debris and worst of all, the shell torn cathedral. It is a mutilated work of art; a sight of which makes our men more anxious to crush its despoiler. Germany must pay for her awful mistreatment of Albert, Ypres and other once beautiful cities. [1/9/17]

The above passage was written a year after the events described. The following one was written on Willie's twenty-first birthday. In those days twenty-one was the official coming of age, when children became adults. He was therefore technically a child for the first two-and-a-half years of his active service, as were hundreds of thousands of other boys who were not so lucky and had already lost their lives.

The Germans have smashed up the whole countryside in some places. The confusion is indescribable. We passed the sites of towns and villages where the debris was so pounded as to obliterate all trace of pre-war activity. Whole districts are so ploughed and churned with shellfire that you cannot even walk between the craters. Fritz still malignantly pounds the ruins but does little military damage. [22/1/18]

There was much more freedom of movement for the troops after the Armistice and Willie was to see more devastation in the aftermath of the shelling from both sides. There was no longer any requirement to conceal where he was; he was based at the RAMC headquarters in St Amand:

We are now at Coupigny, having made our way here from St Amand yesterday. We passed through several towns including Lens. Here was ruin indescribable. It is absolutely impossible to damage Lens more completely than has been done. It is nothing more than a vast, untidy, chaotic, pathetic, miserable and derelict heap of rubbish. If five hundred naval guns bombarded it again from now until this time next year the contours would be altered a little but it would still be only a great heap of broken bricks and concrete and wood. Recently the rubbish heap has been parted in the middle to make a way through and it is touching in the extreme to notice the valiant efforts of some of the old citizens to re-inhabit the lifeless lump called Lens. There are butchers shops, estaminets and so on. Other more ambitious souls have made shanties from the old wood, bricks, new tarred felt and corrugated iron scrounged from the British. [22/4/19]

The town of Nieux les Mines has suffered little damage since our last visit but the workshop billet where eight of our men slept has had such a one that makes us happy it arrived after our departure. The shell apparently entered the window of the room where Kilburn and two others used to sleep, came through the bedroom floor and burst when passing through the ground floor, making havoc of the cellar. Our luck! [25/4/19]

Frustrated by the delay in demobilisation, Willie, now with three stripes on his arm, was still at work among the rubble, checking out sanitary arrangements over a wide area eight months after the Armistice:

I am now situated under canvas at Lacon. An occasional wall here and there and a heap of stones are the only signs that a village ever existed. I am employed visiting all camps within a radius of about five miles and get around on a push bike. [5/6/19]

It is an amazing tribute to the resilience of mankind that all these places were rebuilt and flourished within a few short years.

8

Aerial Warfare

It can truly be said that aerial warfare began in the First World War.

There were the German airships, or Zeppelins, which were used both for reconnaissance and bombing. Defensive measures against this threat were taken in London, in particular the installation of searchlights and the protection of public buildings. A few bombs were dropped on the capital but little damage was done, and this form of warfare was eventually doomed to failure because of the slow speed of the airships and the inherent danger of their inflammable gas bags. Germany did develop airship technology between the wars and used the ships like ocean liners, notably between Germany and America, which cut the six-day boat journey to two days. They were also used for military intelligence; the first true spy aircraft, the famous Graf Zeppelin, was frequently seen over Britain in the late 1930s taking aerial photographs of strategic sites. The tragic fire on the passenger-carrying Hindenberg, with total loss of life of those onboard, effectively demonstrated that airships would not be a priority for military expenditure.

Then there were the first bomber aeroplanes, again developed by the Germans. The Taube was their principal aircraft in this category and it was used to bomb the British positions in France during the First World War. It was a clumsy machine, and its range was short so that it was only used experimentally against London.

German reconnaissance planes did have an important role to play in mapping trench positions, and gun emplacements and balloons were used extensively for the same purpose by both sides.

Most famously there were the fighter planes, the British bi-plane Sopwith Camel and the German tri-planes made famous by the air ace von Richthofen, the 'Red Baron', and his fellow pilot Hermann Goering, who was to become chief of the Luftwaffe and deputy to Hitler in the Second World War. The dog fights between these aircraft became legendary and made marvellous news for the press as they created instant heroes. They also became the subject of highly romanticised fiction in the form of the best-selling 'Biggles' novels of Captain W. E. Johns. The reality was much less glamorous, and in the later part of the war the average life expectancy of fighter pilots was three weeks.

The potential of aeroplanes in warfare was demonstrated so clearly that development between the wars was a major priority to the extent that the Second World War saw Wellington, York and Lancaster bombers, Spitfire and Hurricane fighters plus a host of other specialised aircraft on the British side and the Heinkel and Junkers bombers, the Stuka dive-bomber and the Messerschmitt fighter plus reconnaissance and transport aircraft on the German side.

From his position in the war zone, Willie had ample opportunity to observe the early use of military aircraft and was lucky to avoid death or injury in more than one bombing incident:

I know what it is to be under bomb-dropping aeroplanes. I know what it is to be in an open space without any cover and at the very moment when the Taube seems exactly overhead to hear the rattling buzz of a descending bomb. I have stood petrified and mechanically counted the seconds occupied in the descent then – crash! – and the bomb has burst about a hundred yards away. Of course, you will be aware that the aeroplane raids are but a sideline in our fireworks display, shells are more plentiful. Mortar attacks (Hammenwerfer) are enchanting spectacles to the safely distant observer. Rifle and machine gun bullets make a pretty little sound – phwing! – but there is nothing pretty about the sound of an approaching bomb. [14/6/17]

I went to X yesterday and it was a trifle hot. There were dozens of aeroplanes about and one or two Bosche began to drop bombs. One is forewarned of a bomb by a whistling whizzing sound which is very like the sound of a cart with iron rimmed wheels driving at tremendous speed through a cobbled street in an empty town. Then – bang! – the whole earth trembles and seems to roll under one's feet. A Taube dropped four bombs in succession not more than two hundred yards from us. Shortly afterwards I counted fourteen shells and, incredibly as it may appear, ten of these were duds. [14/2/16]

The other day we had a near escape. A German aeroplane was scouting overhead and our anti-aircraft guns were firing at it. Three bombs fell almost directly on our hut. They did not burst or we should have known about it. As it was they fell with a 'phut' on the soft ground and it was not long before they were dug up as souvenirs. [8/1/16]

There has been much shelling by aeroplanes lately and the other day, about noon, we heard the humming sound which forewarns one of a shell and a projectile fell not far away in the next field. It did not explode but buried itself about six feet in the ground. Nobody was hurt so all was well. [21/1/16]

There seems to have been no bomb disposal procedure in place and the thought of the risk involved in digging up unexploded bombs makes one shudder! The bombs in a raid not long afterwards proved not to be duds, with tragic consequences, though the 41st Section continued to have the devil's own luck:

Two days ago I was rudely awakened from sweet dreams of Blighty by the hum of enemy planes and the harsh rattle of descending bombs. Ten bombs dropped in as many seconds, the nearest being some fifteen yards away from where I lay in bed. Had the ground not been so soft under a thin coating of frost we should have copped out. Another bomb dropped on the adjoining camp, which is about a hundred yards away, and unfortunately killed one man and wounded two others. It also killed three mules.

All these grim incidents have their humorous moments and ours was in the manner that Woolfe darted under his little bed. The funny part is that even if the bed had offered any protection, which is ridiculous, Woolfe only had his head and shoulders underneath it. [27/3/16].

How terrible the last German air raid was. We are compensated little by news of our success on the Messines–Ypres line. Why don't we take reprisals? If the Tommies were asked to vote on the question there would be no doubt about their opinion [17/6/17]

Although Willie thought that they could be effective, the anti-aircraft guns seem to have been generally unsuccessful:

This morning, whilst watching the bombardment of aeroplanes we saw twenty or thirty shots burst all at once round the plane then, shortly after, another group of shells burst. To me this seems the likeliest way of bringing planes down. [21/1/16]

Although I have been out here five long months and have seen aeroplanes being shelled almost daily I have never seen one, whether ours or enemy, hit or brought down. I will give you an idea of what one sees when an aeroplane is being shelled. His attention is first attracted by the popping sound of the anti-aircraft shells bursting. On looking upwards one can see many blobs of white which appear about the size of a small pea. After careful observation one notes that one of the white specks is moving. That is the plane. One then watches the bursting of the shells, which sometimes go up ten at a time, with some interest, but the plane continues saucily to fly about, to all appearances unperturbed. [16/2/16]

Being a pilot was a glamorous occupation, probably because of the danger involved and there was an inevitable daredevil approach by some of the pilots in training and in battle. Perhaps there was also a bit of showing off to those on the ground. The following graphic description of aerobatics was accompanied by a sketch in the letter showing one pilot executing a barrel roll:

Speaking of aeroplanes, the Germans are simply not in it with us in the air. Occasionally, in the night, I take myself away to some high ground which overlooks an aerodrome nearby and am thrilled and delighted by the wonderful evolutions and revolutions our pilots practice. Perhaps there are a dozen in the air at once, diving, swooping sideways, shooting upwards and performing most fantastic feats. There is one plane in particular whose pilot must be entirely without nerve. He loops the loop with ease but most of all he turns right over sideways. To see these tricks performed when fighting the enemy is more exciting than you can understand. [28/7/17]

The French and German pilots were also not above a bit of showboating:

A huge French warplane, or battle plane as these big flying machines are called, lost its way and descended at dusk in the next field to our huts. I saw it rise and depart and perform some pretty evolutions this morning. That incident and a flock of sixteen aeroplanes passing overhead have been the only diverting incidents during the last few days. [9/5/16]

We had an exciting ten minutes yesterday afternoon. A Taube suddenly swooped down like an eagle to its prey, carried out some manoeuvre and flew around our heads so low that we could feel the sweep of his wings and even see the pilot. If excitement is the breath of life we are certainly living extravagantly. [19/9/17]

Perhaps the most flamboyant pilot Willie witnessed was a Frenchman:

The aeroplanes have been badly shelled today. One in particular was very daring. Although immediately over the lines the plane flew very low, almost low enough, I should imagine, to be within range of rifle fire. On observing this risky business, some of the fellows who had been breathlessly watching the plane, expecting no doubt to see it brought down at any moment, said that its pilot must be the 'French Major'. If any brilliant or risky feat is performed it is the Major. It is said that on a very windy day a few weeks ago he ascended and flew over the German lines. Because of the strong wind he was unable to return, try as he may. Report says that, nothing daunted, he flew to Holland and returned when the weather conditions were more favourable. [12/1/16]

A rather touching family story concerned an air raid later in the war:

I had my first night in a new billet yesterday and – wonder of wonders – slept between sheets in a real bed for the first time in France. It is in a quiet village though our first night here, Sergeant Leslie is with me, was signalled by a little incident. Just as we were preparing for bed we heard the familiar hum of the night birds (Bosch aeroplanes) followed by the reverberating thunder of bombs bursting. Madame, afraid, came to the door and begged us to 'descendre a la maison' where, by the dismal light of one candle, we saw several neighbours all talking rapidly and anxious for relieving words to alleviate their fear. Her little boy, aged about three and in a nightdress, sat on his mother's knee wondering what was the matter. 'Is it bombs mamam', said the youngster. 'No my little one, it is the soldiers practising' said his mother. 'I wish I had a gun' said the boy and so it went on, the prattling of the child helping to dispel their nervousness, eventually enabling us to say 'bon soir' and so to sleep. [13/4/18]

The writer recalls a not dissimilar incident in the Second World War when the sound of aeroplanes flying over the family home in the north of England caused the five-year-old to climb into bed with his father – Willie – and his mother. 'Are they German aeroplanes?' I asked. 'No, they are ours' came the reply, meant to be reassuring. In fact, the distinctive rise and fall of the engine beat, which I had already learnt was the way to identify enemy aircraft, meant that they certainly were German aircraft on their way to bomb Liverpool. The engines of the German bombers were not well synchronised, giving rise to the unmistakeable throbbing sound.

Just one month before the Armistice, Willie had a farewell taste of the German bombers:

I am back at H.Q. after a tiresome and in one particular an exciting journey. The excitement was at B where Fritz welcomed us back in his most unpleasant manner – an air raid. However everything is now serene. [25/9/18]

Aerial warfare, though spectacular, did comparatively little damage in the First World War but its use provided a foretaste of the potential of what has become the principle means of conducting warfare today.

9

Gas Warfare

Gas is a particularly nasty weapon and it was used by the Germans, and the British, with horrific effects. The substance used was mustard gas, and even brief unprotected exposure to it could lead to an agonising choking death; more than a whiff could lead to severe lung damage and blindness. Prolonged contact with the skin caused severe burning. Tragic pictures of lines of blinded men shuffling along in single file, each holding the shoulder of the man in front so that they did not get lost, have featured in many documentary films about the war. They haunt the memory of anyone who has seen them.

The gas weapon could only be used when there was a guarantee of a strong and continuing favourable wind blowing directly from behind the user's lines into the enemy trenches and the territory immediately behind them. The gas quickly dissipated so that it was really only the men actually in the trenches who were at serious risk The danger to the gas user was that any lull or change in wind direction could lead to it drifting back over the user's lines, which is thankfully why there were only rare occasions when gas could be used effectively. Only a few thousand casualties from gas attacks were recorded in the post-war statistics.

The British soldiers were all issued with gas masks, or helmets as they were called, which had to be kept available at all times when near the German lines. The masks were grotesque rubber objects with a tube leading to a canister of neutralising chemical, typically sodium thiosulphate. Later models had the canister fitted directly to the nose of the mask so that there was less to impede the carrying or use of a conventional weapon such as a rifle or hand grenade. The masks were highly effective, although they made the wearers look as though they had come from outer space. If the canister had not been recently replaced, the chemical could be refreshed by urinating on it, and the troops were all instructed in this procedure.

A sequence of letters early in 1916 showed that the Germans were actively using gas. The first of them suggests that intelligence reports had revealed the threat of a major attack, to the degree that the men were issued with two gas masks each:

On Wednesday we were kept in readiness for an expected gas attack. We were given warning and told to sleep with our gas masks near at hand. Sentries and guards were put on duty outside all the huts, tents and other billets and were to give us warning if anything happened. At 4.00 a.m. we were awakened and told to dress and parade with helmets on in the field behind the huts. Brrrr. Helmets were inspected and extra warning given. We were sent back to bed with instructions to wear our first helmet round our necks and keep the second one handy. However nothing happened, fortunately, but we are still on the alert. [8/1/16]

This was a false alarm, but the state of alert continued and Willie gave a vivid description of conditions at the front, with the troops in constant anticipation of a gas attack:

The weather has been wet and cold for the last few days and life has been very uncomfortable. Last night I lay in the tent and expected to wake up thoroughly wet. After three days of almost continual rain the tent somehow sprang a leak and quite near my ear big drops began to fall on the tent board. It was quite dark and the rest of the boys had commenced to snore, some soft, some loud and all through there sounded the pit-pat of dropping water. The drops fell only a few inches from me but the noise seemed so heavy that I thought my comrades would surely be awakened by it but they slept on and in vain did I try to follow their good example. As I lay there I felt glad of my groundsheet, which next to the rifle is surely the soldier's best friend. The tent board sloped down slightly to the tent curtain and fortunately the water did not touch me. Just as I was dropping off all the guns in the neighbourhood commenced to give Fritz a little excitement. Bang, bang went the guns and the shells screamed as they sped on their rapid journey. The wind was pretty strong and was blowing from the trenches, making our tent pole creak with the violence. I put out my hand and drew my gas helmet nearer. One must take no chances if he values his life. If the German chose to send over his deadly gas the wind would speedily carry it down on us. I again snuggled into my blanket and the singing of the shells was my lullaby. I fell asleep and dreamt of home. [11/6/16]

All this took place just before the Battle of the Somme and one wonders if the Germans had counter-intelligence of the build-up of Allied troops and were using gas to disrupt it. The precautions which the Allies were taking proved fully justified, for the real thing occurred a few days later with hideous consequences, though lucky the 41st Section was on the fringes of the attack:

We settled down to sleep at 9.30 p.m. little thinking that we were to get only one or two hours rest. About midnight a bombardment of unusual vigour commenced. The guns roared and dimly we could hear the crack of the machine guns and rifles. We soon realised, for we are well seasoned soldiers by now, that some attack or action was taking place in the line and, observing from the fluttering walls of our tent that the wind was in favour of the Germans and blowing down on us from the trenches, we got up and went outside to see if gas was coming over. The night was fine and clear and although we could see no change in the atmosphere we could distinctly detect an unusual smell. The artillery was working with greater vigour than before, if that were possible and we concluded, rightly as later events proved, that the Germans were making a gas attack. We went back to our blankets and laid awake with our gas masks handy, on the alert for any increase in the smell, when we should have immediately put them on. The rumbling still continued and by the great flashes from some of the bigger guns our tent was illuminated. We heard the old church clock chime one and still the bombardment continued. Shortly after 2 o'clock the strafing ceased and with gas helmet close handy I at any rate was soon fast asleep. [18/6/16]

The following morning brought one of the most harrowing scenes imaginable, when Willie and his comrades witnessed the dreadful procedure of triage on the victims of the gas attack – triage, whereby the medical officers made instant life-or-death decisions on the unfortunates who had been directly in the gas cloud:

The guns were very quiet in the morning and we were all anxious to hear what had happened the night before. It was a glorious morning and seemed so full of life and joy that I began to forget my almost sleepless night and the cause thereof. But I could not forget it for very long for as I reached the village school, now a field ambulance depot and dressing station, I encountered the awful results of the previous night's attack. There, in the old schoolyard, were row upon row of gassed men on stretchers and more were being brought in every minute. The doctors were going along the line, quickly examining the poor fellows and giving relief where they could.

There the soldiers lay under the hot sun with the sweet summer breeze blowing over them. Those that were unconscious seemed to breathe quite easily and but for the greyish hue of their skin one could have imagined that they were in a natural sleep. But the poor fellows who were conscious! They struggled and strained and gasped for air. Some fell from their stretchers in their convulsions. One young soldier a little way down the line was feebly struggling to open his mouth to the fullest extent with his fingers. The doctor came quickly along the line. The men who had received attention were put again on board the motor ambulances and taken away to the base for further treatment. The doctor came to the young soldier and, baring the man's wrist, injected something, morphine or a similar drug. The man ceased to struggle and his breathing seemed easier. On the doctor went to the next, who was lying very still and quiet. He felt his pulse and looked in his eyes. 'Mortuary' curtly said the doctor and two stretcher bearers carried the man into a little outbuilding at the end of the yard where too many of these dead were already lying. They would be buried in the afternoon. Graves were being dug now.

More and more men were brought in and when I left to proceed to my duty several hundred men had been dealt with. The ambulances were running to and fro until 7 or 8 o'clock that night but now everything is comparatively quiet again. The report in the papers will simply say:

'On the night of the umpteenth the Germans launched an attack. They used gas but were unsuccessful in reaching our trenches. The British losses were slight'. [19/6/16]

In carrying out the triage the doctors therefore had three choices: sending saveable men back to base hospital, giving the hopeless cases morphine and leaving them to die without pain, or committing those already dead to the mortuary.

Just five days later the troops were given a lecture – perhaps arranged to salve the consciences of those who had been in charge of the gassed men:

We had a gas lecture today and were instructed in the manner of use of the gas helmet. It is possible, by wearing the helmet in a certain manner, to have it on and be free from danger in three seconds. We were told the signs which mark the approach of gas and also told how to forecast a German gas attack. If these new instructions are faithfully carried out it is absolutely impossible for any man to be gassed unless the helmet is leaking. It is said that the man who invented the new way of wearing the helmet has been given some very high honour, D.S.O. or something similar. Of course, I dare not explain the method but it is wonderfully simple and ingenious. Our Staff Sergeant, who instructed us, has been taught the use of various kinds of helmet and has himself been through gas which was five times as strong as the Germans ever use and he felt no ill effect. [21/6/16]

The Geneva Convention specifically bans the use of poison gas and it is interesting to note that in the classic German novel of the First World War, *All Quiet on the Western Front*, the German soldiers describe an exposure to gas which may have been British or perhaps their own drifting back on a change of wind. In any case, the British were said to have experimented with it during the Second World War in northern Russia, although gas was not used tactically by either side in that war, even though the Germans had developed Zyclon for use in the gas chambers in which millions of Jews perished, victims of Hitler's 'final solution'. Britain had stocks of gas and Winston Churchill had prepared provisional orders for its use in certain circumstances. By now, technology had moved on and mustard gas had been superseded by nerve gases, which could paralyse the entire nervous system.

The staff sergeant had obviously undergone his gassing experience in a controlled test of the helmets during his instruction, to demonstrate their effectiveness in a practical rather than theoretical way.

The threat of gas attacks on Britain itself was such during the Second World War that every man, woman and child was issued with a gas mask, normal black pattern for older children and adults and less-hideous-looking red rubber ones called 'Mickey Mouse' masks for younger children. Babies were issued with large, incubator-like contraptions into which an adult had to pump air manually through the chemical pads. Schoolchildren went to school with masks in their cases and hung them on their pegs in the cloakroom. When they were handed in after the war in 1945, the whole floor of the assembly hall in the West Yorkshire primary school attended by the writer was covered with masks of all three types.

It is interesting to note, well after the end of the Second World War, in the personal experience of the writer, that National Service conscripts in the Royal Air Force were all given gas lectures and then forced to march, unprotected, in a gas chamber, round an open canister of tear gas, singing a popular song of the day – 'The Happy Wanderer' – to make sure that it was impossible to hold ones breath. Then, choking and with eyes streaming, they were led out into the open air to recover. Tear gas is unpleasant and totally debilitating during exposure but has no long-term effects. It has been widely used for riot control by many nations.

10

Philosophy of War and Peace

The non-commissioned ranks contained large numbers of intelligent, thoughtful men, from backgrounds unlikely to lead to selection as officers in the class-ridden society of the early twentieth century. It is not surprising that thoughts and conversations were often of a philosophical nature. All the men shared a hatred of the Germans and at times believed in a swift end to the conflict, but the wider issues of war and peace and their effect on serving men were often discussed and questions raised about the conduct of the war.

The 41st Section had more than its share of well-educated men and had an interesting introduction to the justification of war during initial training in London:

I am writing this in the central YMCA where we have had a splendid talk this afternoon. The speaker ridiculed the idea of international intercession through prayer saying that people praying on one particular Sunday felt they had done quite a bit for the war, whilst they tolerated all sorts of sins without demur so that national praying made us nationally hypocritical. He then turned to the justification of war from a Christian standpoint very nicely. I think you would have enjoyed hearing him. [15/8/15]

After two years of active service Willie set out his hopes and beliefs in some detail:

Business as usual was the cry in 1914, but now, business and pleasure and even one's very existence is controlled so that the terrible machinery of war may be oiled, repaired, increased and kept in ceaseless motion, though I realise that the aim of this activity is that the war will sooner stop. What can the men who are left (how sad is this last phrase) do after the war? Will they make every effort to regain their old civilian occupation or will they seek outdoor occupations where their new found freedom will perhaps be more obvious? Will it have worsened men's morals? With regard to political parties, which faction will have increased its support after the war? [1/9/17]

His conclusion was that most of the survivors, certainly the less well educated, would have had all ambition stifled by their experience and would have but one desire: to get back to the very streets of their origin and extract every ounce of pleasure from their return to their old lives. As regards the political question which he himself had raised, Willie showed remarkable foresight in his realisation that men would no longer be satisfied with the old establishment politics:

Which political faction will have increased its supporters because of the war? My own answer will have become obvious to you for I think that the Socialist, or Labour party will have gained more support. [1/9/17]

There were also interesting thoughts on conventional morality, remembering that the war started at a time when strict Victorian attitudes were still the norm of British society:

What effect will the war have on morality? On the face of it morals will have deteriorated. Men have perhaps become accustomed to taking drink, talking foully and acting coarsely but on consideration I think you will agree that these shortcomings are likely to disappear when home influences become apparent once again. No, the war will have had an uplifting moral effect. A brotherly help one another feeling will have developed and many will cease to prate about religion and become more practical in their goodness, thereby decreasing hypocrisy. [1/9/17]

What wonderful things men have done since war began. They have voluntarily faced death for a principle. If you had told a young man before the war that he would risk death rather than be a hypocrite he would have laughed, but particularly since the Compulsory Service Act men have been doing this daily. When conscription arrived there was the provision for appeals and developing all sorts of conscientious reasons to escape service by telling lies. But apart from a few contemptibles they protested not and allowed themselves to be taken into the army. It is really remarkable and wonderful and glorious isn't it? [17/2/17]

There was always the hope that the end of the war was in sight. Willie penned this piece of sustained metaphor in the middle of 1917:

Perhaps we will all be home this winter. Perhaps the war will burst like a thunderstorm, rapidly and unexpectedly. Maybe the clouds have nearly passed and the so long-hidden sun will burst on us just as rapidly and when that sunshine of peace is upon us, awakening the seed of pleasure and comfort which so many of us had to bury when war broke out, we shall all feel full of life and joy once more. We shall all be much happier. You will say 'no, not all for many have been bereaved' but even those who have lost their dearest will be gladdened once more. Moreover the allies will have been victorious and the stricken mothers and wives will feel their men did not die in vain. [27/7/17]

An example of pure lateral thinking came in a letter recalling the traumatic experience of being transported while still only eighteen years old from the ordered safety of Britain to the war zone. It showed just how this experience turned boys into men:

The journey from England to France made that the worst day of my life – but was it the worst day? Perhaps, viewed from some standpoints it was the best day. A new world lay before me and me still a boy, eighteen years old and fighting my own and my country's battles and it has done me good. Jack London was an oyster catcher; he ran away to sea and then wrote. Robert Blatchford was in a spinning mill in Halifax; he joined the army and wrote. Fighting their own battles did them good. It has done me good. Experience is a fine teacher and I will remember what difficulty I had in penning a letter to Blighty and now I seem to write and write. Not much in comparison to London and Blatchford but oh what a lot for William Whittaker. [19/7/19]

I am young, I am healthy. I am seeing different things, observing different customs. I have embarked on a great adventure, a temporary new life. Although I grumble, every soldier does, deep down in my heart I am enjoying this experience better than anything which has occurred in my hitherto uneventful life. [8/12/15]

The popular journalist and pedagogue Horatio Bottomley was ever ready to pontificate about the war and was no doubt regarded as a reliable source of opinion by his readers and audience in Britain. There was a different view from the trenches!

I have just read with interest Horatio Bottomley's latest article in which he says 'I have been in hell and from its depths have seen the shining splendour of heaven. In the scorched and blackened track of the Devil I have met with God'. What a splendid jeu de mots, what fine journalism. He says he has been in hell – yes, for seven days. Why, it is more than seven hundred days of hell which I have suffered. Some of those days, when duty has taken me into the line along with the infantrymen, the only shining splendours of heaven which I have experienced among the men are thoughts of Blighty – home! Material things count out here, a quiet sleep, good food, bodily comfort of any description. It is all very well

*for Bottomley to spend seven days in hell and then go back
to London to sit in his warm room at his desk writing of
the perfect harmony of heaven which he has discovered
while walking over the devastated Somme battlefield. Good
journalism indeed – pooh, it makes you ill. [25/10/17]*

The poignancy of the only heaven being back home in Blighty,
so evident in his condemnation of the armchair pundit
Bottomley, was nowhere better expressed than in a touching
comment which might be thought sentimental if taken out of
context of the real horror of the battlefield:

*I went to see the show by the Tonies last night and had a most
enjoyable evening. I was as interested in the audience as the
troupe. The light comedian sang 'Pack up your troubles in
your old kit bag' and I sang and laughed with the rest of them,
notwithstanding the lump in my throat, but when I lay in bed
last night I thought how really pathetic these little incidents
are. 'Smile, smile, smile' runs the song and Tommy laughed
and laughed and showed how completely he can pack up his
troubles – and what troubles he has; active acquaintance with
Fritz, mud, lice and discomfort of every description. Britain,
thy sons are wonderful.*

*What about those other songs. 'Take me back to dear old
Blighty', 'I want to go home', 'Blighty, Blighty, please put
me on the Blighty line'. These are not meaningless ditties to
Tommy, they are prayers. To hear a thousand soldier boys
singing them brings a lump to your throat and tears to
your eyes. I suppose you will call me sentimental. Perhaps*

I am, for I feel sure that if a band were cruel enough to play 'Home sweet home' I should sob, and not alone. [26/8/16]

Exactly three years after he had joined up Willie summed up the optimism of the early days of the conflict, so heartbreakingly to be dashed by events. The three-year term was highly significant as that had been the specific minimum the early volunteers signed up for:

The war has not taken away our power of looking back. Our memories, except in a few cases where shock has deprived a fellow of that fine power which enables him to bring to his mind's eye the picture of his home and dear ones and of those happy pre-war days whose merits he has only appreciated since this war began. Three years ago I was in London, anxiously hoping to pass the military doctor and be pronounced fit and eager to don khaki for three years or the duration of the war. What quibbling there was about the first part of that phrase. Why. The war was going to finish in about six months. Did that phrase have a deep meaning that if the war finished in six months we were to be kept in until three years had expired? We were patriotic enough, we wanted to be soldiers, but hang it all we only wanted to serve for the duration. Why the mention of three years when everybody knew, including Horatio Bottomley, that it was only a matter of a few months before Fritz would be down and out? Well, we all knew didn't we? Yet here we are, the luckier of us, still heading our letters 'Somewhere in France'. [2/6/18]

Willie recalled the 'dream' which had seen him brought before the censor to be severely reprimanded for writing about peace on earth and goodwill to all men, including German men. It seems astonishing to the reader a century later that the charming and indeed noble thoughts expressed in the description of its effects on all the soldiers should have been regarded as subversive by the authorities:

Now, that is all very well for a dream but who can imagine Fritz as a peace lover? and moreover who can imagine Tommy the peace lover until Attila has been driven back into his own country? [9/12/16]

Although nobody knew it, the war had only five more months to run when the previous letter was written, but far from being released when the duration of the conflict came to an end, Willie was to be kept in the Army for a further eight months after the Armistice, leaving him feeling badly let down by the demobilisation system.

11

Billets

The accommodation of soldiers on active service in the First World War was very different from that in the organised camps and barracks with all modern conveniences which are regarded as normal and necessary for the armies of today.

The arrangements for recruits in Britain during training were quite reasonable of course but the transition to France and Belgium was a rude shock. Nights were spent on the stone floors of animal pens, huddled in greatcoats and blankets. The infantry spent much time in the trenches, living in dugouts formed in the very trenches themselves with perhaps a piece of corrugated iron as a roof with mud or sandbags on top and, if they were lucky, planks, known as trench boards, as a floor. Rest for these troops when they were given a spell out of the line was in tented camps set, during rainy periods, in a sea of mud.

Junior officers in the trenches had to make do with dugouts, the better-equipped ones of course, but otherwise officers, almost invariably, had the pick of civilian housing and if you were a general you might live in a commandeered chateau surrounded by uniformed servants. No wonder some commentators have accused the High Command of being out of touch with the reality in the front line.

The other ranks were not so fortunate though the boys who were to form the nucleus of the 41st Section had comfortable accommodation during their initial training at Chelsea barracks, nowadays the home of the famous Army pensioners. They were actually billeted in a former Methodist chapel nearby, but with proper beds in dormitories. Then on field training in Hampshire they were in houses, though with many men to a room.

It was a different story in the war zone, with the men having to put up with whatever was available, even including barns and pigsties, and even being abandoned without billet at all by their NCOs.

Our officer has been very considerate and has done his best for us ever since he came out. I remember at Bouvray we were sitting in some motor ambulances for many hours during which time it rained unceasingly. Our N.C.Os, who had been instructed to find us a hot drink and a billet, had selfishly found a billet for themselves at 9.00 p.m. and quietly gone to sleep. At about 2.00 a.m., having huddled in our blankets all that time, our officer came up and was astonished to find us still there. He immediately found us some hot tea and a billet. [15/1/16]

Although usually better housed than the infantry, the 41st Section had its share of living in dugouts in the trenches:

I am now on duty in a different area and unable to visit my civilian friends and enjoy the usual musicale. I am a good way away, being billeted underground and in the trenches. If my correspondence is brief you will understand that it cannot be helped. My present comrade is Salter and we two are billeted with the infantry. We are however as safe as possible under the circumstances, and I may be relieved very shortly. [5/2/17]

Not all dugouts were miserable holes, though many of those actually in the trenches merited that description. Even a dugout could be turned into quite a good billet:

I am now situated in the midst of a great wilderness with no houses or civilisation in sight. I have a nice little dugout all to myself. It is fairly well lit and ventilated. The floor is boarded and the walls are covered in canvas. I have a little bed and after a beautiful bit of wangling I am in possession of four blankets, which are none too many for it strikes rather damp below ground. The real drawback is the rats. At this very moment I can hear them squeaking and scurrying around behind the iron roof. Still, c'est la guerre. [10/7/17]

They were often in tents, sometimes draughty, sometimes leaking, but occasionally, when the tent had not been heavily used, it could be the better end of the accommodation they had to put up with. An example of the worst that tented accommodation could offer was related after the Battle of the Somme:

I wrote a letter last year in a leaky tent near Dernacourt where we were resting after a dose of Somme. It was there that we had the 'pleasant' experience of seeing our blankets and kit floating about in six inches of water inside the tent. Our camp was pitched on low ground and a heavy rainstorm had caused this flood within a short hour. Woe unto us for we slept not at all that night but walked about to pass the time. [1/9/17]

Then the contrast:

There are seven of us in this sub-section and we are exceptionally comfy. I and three others are billeted in a brand new tent, a lucky stroke, complete with floor boards. We also have made beds of a sort and, having lately received our extra winter blankets, we are quite alright. The others sleep in a small iron shanty also in beds. They are beds to us although you may be at a loss what to call them. They are wire netting stretched across a wooden frame, that is all. Of course we have no mattresses but the wire 'gives' where we, or more particularly I, protrude and well, it is better than sleeping on, de cold cold ground. [?1917]

'De cold cold ground' was a quotation from a popular Negro spiritual.

Even very humble accommodation but with a proper roof overhead seemed first rate compared to some billets they had to put up with:

This billet is just about the most comfortable we have ever had. You would be very amused to see us when we are laid down at night. We utilise almost all the floor space. I will illustrate it with a rough diagram. [?1918]

The sketch was with the letter and shows a hut with a fireplace, two separate rooms for the sergeants and eight men in the main room, with Willie in the corner. There seem to have been no beds and it was more normal than not for men to sleep on the floor, or bare earth protected only by a groundsheet. Even the 'rest' accommodation provided in the elegant hotels and boarding houses on the Marine Parade at Folkestone, for men awaiting boats to France on their return from leave, was completely unfurnished. If they wanted to lie down it was on the floor!

Wherever they were billeted it was of necessity impermanent as the section was regularly on the move to tackle different assignments. Sometimes they slept on bare earth and at others had straw paliasses, but rarely proper bedding, just a groundsheet, blankets and their clothing! They were resourceful, however, and there were minor concessions to relieve some of the hardship:

There has been heavy rain but so far we have suffered little beyond mud as our tents are well pitched on the top of a hill. We have been supplied with winter caps of an exceptionally warm material, with thick chinstraps which cover the ears, and also with long waterproof capes. The great value of these will be understood when I tell you that the greatcoat is used by all as an extra night covering during the cold weather. One or two of us have made little beds, which just lift us from the damp floor, so that with my two blankets – I managed to pick up an extra one a short time ago, to nobody's detriment I am pleased to say – and my greatcoat and last but not least my splendid air pillow I sleep well and comfortable and warm. We shall be supplied later with thick gloves and other winter necessaries. [17/10/15]

The air pillow had been sent from home in a food parcel. That first winter showed how they made the very best of it and coped relatively well. Fire precautions were obviously pretty lax or non-existent:

I for one sleep very warm. We have a little coke brazier which we bring into the tent all hot at about 6.00 p.m. The fire keeps alight until about 10 o'clock. I do not take my underpants off nor my socks at night and my first blanket I pull round me and fasten up with straps. Then on goes my greatcoat and after that another blanket which I also strap round my feet and then I pull over me a long thick sack. We find little dodges to keep warm here. [9/11/15]

Recounted a generation later to his family Willie recalled the practice of 'threeing up' which was used in extremely cold conditions on groundsheets laid on the bare earth under canvas. To make best use of the limited blanket ration the men would share between three of them, lying side by side with four of five blankets on top. The favourite position was in the middle where there was extra body warmth, and they used to claim this in turns.

Sometimes there was a real roof over their heads, though the description of one billet in an abandoned village as a house was perhaps a little exaggerated.

The weather is very hot and sunny and all of us are again assuming the tan of a haymaker. I am feeling très bon. We are now billeted in an attic, sans windows and here and there sans tiles, of a dilapidated old farmhouse. All the village is in a similar state of decay. In decay but not in ruins, comprenez? [28/7/16]

Reading between the lines it appears that the above farmhouse had not actually been shelled but on at least three occasions their billets were destroyed by German shells and the boys sometimes had to make do with shelter in broken-down houses:

This is a wonderfully pretty French village. There are not too many soldiers here to prevent us seeing the civilians. We are billeted in a dilapidated cottage and are really comfortable. [8/9/17]

We are not living in dugouts but our house, into whose roof and upper rooms more than one shell has poked his unwelcome nose, is heavily sandbagged all round and no-one is allowed to live above the ground floor. In this same village some of the billets are cellars but if it is at all safe to live above ground we do so for comfort's sake. [2/3/17]

The little dodges which Willie had referred to became real invention, and on another occasion they showed their considerable resourcefulness in creating a home far from home.

I am now living with Phillips in a little house constructed from groundsheets, several empty ammunition boxes and a sheet of corrugated iron. Although no more than three feet high it is as comfortable and cosy a little kip as I have known for some time. [9/8/16]

Sometimes they were in much better billets. For example at one time they were in a proper house, with proper beds and even clean sheets, lodging with a family. Madame cooked for the lodgers and supplemented their Army rations, often at no charge. On another occasion Willie described a wooden hut commanding magnificent views and then later in the war a large house with a pond which members of the section were able to use as a swimming pool.

We are billeted very comfortably just now. We have made beds of a sort and we are more cosy than is often possible on active service. I am writing this on a useful, if not ornamental table and am sitting on a form which we managed to pick up in a billet recently vacated. We have become quite expert at picking up useful necessaries. [14/3/17]

So, Tommy moved from accommodation to accommodation, often after only a brief stay, with dignified acceptance, making the best of whatever was available. It is astonishing that, with all their privations, the men remained cheerful and just got on with the job of defeating the enemy.

12

Food, Glorious Food

Besides fundamentally resolving the most serious health and hygiene problems with the consequent reduction in deaths from bad sanitation, the authorities had learnt the other main lesson from previous wars, that proper food not only made troops fitter and better able to contribute to the fight but it also improved morale enormously.

It is evident that the diet of a soldier in France, though limited, was nutritious and plentiful, although lacking five servings of fruit and vegetables a day. It was based on corned beef, or bully beef as it was known, biscuits, bacon, tea, sugar and jam. This was supplemented in various ways by the ingenuity of the troops themselves, by food parcels from home and the availability of food in the many bar/restaurant estaminets in towns and villages behind the lines which soldiers used when resting from their duties.

This is in stark contrast to the fare of German soldiers, so well described in the famous novel *All Quiet on the Western Front*; towards the end of the war there was not enough food to go round. Indeed, it is held by many historians that it was shortages of food for the troops and even greater ones domestically which forced Germany to agree to end hostilities in 1918.

The basic satisfaction of Tommy with the overall quality and quantity of their food was well evident:

I have been living on rations for two years now and I very seldom feel hungry or improperly nourished. Of course, the daintiness of the food is not up to civilian standards but I do not doubt that it is more wholesome and that is what matters. I really think that it would be a good thing for the country to be put on rations. [25/2/17]

I heard an officer answer a question as to the state of mind of Tommy by saying 'It all depends on rations. If they are good Tommy is optimistic. If they are bad —.' [12/7/17]

Not that food supplies at home in England were without problems, and Willie at one stage suggested that the parcels should not contain food, or at least be reduced in number, because of shortages caused in part by the success of German U-boats in sinking merchant shipping:

By the way, things seem to be very dear in England and if you like you could send a parcel fortnightly instead of weekly. We are never short of food unless there is some traffic delay and even then we are not actually short. The only difference is that we have bully and biscuits instead of fresh meat and bread. [14/3/17]

The suggestion was predictably ignored and the parcels continued at a rate even more frequent than weekly.

During initial training in London, Willie repeatedly stated how physically well he was and the midday meal given to the recruits during a 20-mile route march may well have been typical:

This consisted of cold meat straight from the joint, pickles and bread cut into chunks about three inches thick, all of which went down, fat and all. We then had two apples and rested for two hours. For drink we had water drawn from a nearby running ditch, sterilised and purified by men from the Corps. [15/6/15]

Dinners in the barracks were just as substantial:

We have as much good meat as we want, potatoes, beans and pudding afterwards, sometimes currant or tapioca or duff. [11/7/15]

There were plenty of free food offerings in London for soldiers in training or passing through on the rare leaves from France. These were church or servicemen's institutes or charitable ventures set up by the ladies of the city as a way of doing their bit for the war. The normal offering was tea and cakes, or wads as they were known, but Willie hit the jackpot one day:

We went down to Victoria and, wonders never cease, blundered into a place which provides free for soldiers tea and coffee, with cheese, meat and fish sandwiches ad lib as often as you like. [15/6/15]

We went to the YMCA headquarters in Tottenham Court Road, attended service and were then served with free tea which was all the more satisfying because of the white linen and also because of the attention we received. [21/6/15]

During their war games in Hampshire, the section was under canvas and eating field rations for the first time:

We are now feeding on dog biscuits, which are really not bad, and bully beef, which is tasty if a little salty. [25/8/15]

During his four years in France Willie never once complained about the Army food, and in any case the parcels from his parents, frequently including gifts from relatives and friends, usually contained food, as well as comforts such as cigarettes and toiletries. The regular food items were sweets, cake and sauces to flavour the bully beef. Exotic items such as meat pie and cooked chicken were sent on special occasions. The fact that the food arrived still fresh demonstrated the speed of the postal service, which seems normally to have taken a couple of days only from Lancashire to France. The parcels were always shared with immediate comrades, and even soldiers who did not have such thoughtful relatives as Willie – though his was not a wealthy family – would have a good dietary supplement from the parcels of their pals. From the contents of some parcels, however, you might have thought that Tom and Bella Whittaker were regular patrons of the Burnley equivalent of Fortnum & Mason:

The beautiful tin of lobster made tea much more enjoyable and the sight of a tin of strawberries gave me pleasant thoughts. It sounds rather greedy discussing food in this manner but out here man becomes much more of an animal than in civil life. It is only natural. [15/1/16]

On another occasion an evening routine was recounted:

At about 9.30 p.m. we make bread and butter and hot cocoa. Together with the chicken you sent and some cake you can judge that we do not fare badly. [9/11/15]

In keeping with the noble tradition of that organisation, the YMCA always tried to set up an establishment wherever soldiers were on active service. North-eastern France was no exception:

These last two days I have been working near a large YMCA place and the kind officer there has provided tea and cakes ad lib at any time during the day. [13/5/16]

Army rations were sometimes supplemented by local fare:

The weather is glorious and I am still carrying on with the early cold bath, bacon and egg for breakfast and a bottle of Guinness for supper mode of life. I feel absolutely in the pink. I am sorry to hear that your food quantities and quality are a trifle unsatisfactory but for your consolation let me say that Tommy is doing rather well. The soldier's bread ration is about seven lbs. a week. His meat ration is about as much.

Vegetables are becoming daily more plentiful. For tomorrow's dinner we are to be regaled on rabbit. One rabbit between three men is the ration and I contend this is very generous fare. In addition to this good food we have been able to get rhubarb for dinner nearly every other day. This has been a gift to us from some of the civilians and is not a ration. On rhubarbless days we have enjoyed boiled rice, which is a ration, and given a fair amount of jam, marmalade, butter, or rather margarine, pickles, raisins, currants, dates etc. These rations are universal throughout the army in the fighting area. [3/6/17]

On a grimmer note the troops had to carry a pack of iron rations, which they were forbidden to eat except under orders to do so because nothing else was available:

If we lose our iron rations we shall be charged five francs, just over four shillings. When I come home on leave you shall see my iron rations and I think you will agree they are not worth more than one shilling: four dog biscuits, a tin of bully, one Oxo cube and a tablespoonful of tea and sugar. [20/3/16]

When they were behind the line the boys were able to visit the local estaminets for a meal, where the favourite choice was egg and chips, affordable even on the meagre pay of a private. Fruit trees were raided in season, with or without the permission of the farmers, though the locals seemed to be generally happy to allow these depredations. Willie recollected, in a letter a year after the Battle of the Somme, how wonderful the bonus of local fruit could be:

From the man-made hell of the Somme we went, and were rested in mind and body to Ailly, a typical French village just out of the path of the war, where apples, pears and other fruit grew in profusion. It was ours for the picking unless Madame, or a Military Policeman, was about but of course they would have needed a thousand eyes to have always kept Tommy in view. [1/9/17]

Occasionally there were even better treats, probably at the cost of a few cigarettes:

I have also regaled myself on strawberries not many days past. By using bribery and corruption and a little broken French flattery or tact on a chateau jardinière I succeeded in winning some of those succulent fruits – yum. [17/8/17]

Long after the war the story of an unaccustomed addition to the diet was told to Willie's family. The section was billeted on farmland where the proprietor kept ducks. Every night a designated member of the section would creep into the ducks' shed and purloin any eggs newly laid. Glorious egg breakfasts were eaten for several days before the farmer was overheard telling his wife that the ducks had stopped laying and would have to be slaughtered. The language was readily understood as most of the men learned kitchen French quite quickly. The boys stopped stealing forthwith but whether this brought about a reprieve for the ducks or they ended up on the table was never discovered.

Another food bonus in the autumn came from the horse lines. There were nearly as many horses as men in some camps, not only the thoroughbreds of the cavalry and officers but the draught horses and pack mules used for hauling artillery, supply wagons and so forth. The vast quantities of manure were raked neatly, with good Army tidiness, into long mounds and in the autumn these yielded enormous crops of mushrooms which must have made a delicious supplement to the morning bacon.

Meals when in camp were mostly prepared by Army cooks, and although the rations were good the macabre sense of humour of Tommy did not prevent one of these cooks acquiring the nickname 'Vomit' – which he seems to have answered to without rancour! When billeted only as a small section there was not the luxury of a dedicated cook, so the boys had to designate one of their number. Willie recounted one of his spells as cook, which was taken in turn by the men of the section for a week at a time:

An army cook has no gas stoves or special fire grates and has only one size of cooking dish provided. Of course, petrol tins can also be pressed into service. The worst thing about cooking is that it is always terribly black and dirty. It does not need a Sherlock Holmes to distinguish a permanent cook. His clothes speak: they are black. Furthermore a cook must rise in the morning about an hour before his comrades to prepare their breakfast. [1/10/16]

With some pride Willie described two days' menus he had served up during one of his spells as section cook:

Yesterday
Breakfast. Eggs and bacon: Coffee: Bread butter and jam.
Dinner. Soup: steak and onions: Cabbage: Potatoes: Rice
pudding.
Tea. Bread: Butter: Jam: Tea

Today
Breakfast: Boiled eggs; cocoa etc.
Dinner: Bully beef: Machonnochies stew: Potatoes: Cabbage:
Tomatoes.
Tea: As before.

Later on we had fruit, salmon or sardines. We rarely live up
to this standard but are never starved. [7/10/16]

He was glad when his duties as cook were over, however!
Special occasions meant special food. The Christmas dinners
were the highlight and the troops were delighted to partake
of the following meal on Christmas Day 1915:

We borrowed plates, glasses, tables, chairs etc. from a café
opposite and made our little room quite pleasant with coloured
plants and evergreens. Our officers were present and we had
a very merry time. I enclose the menu which Martin designed
and though the fun will weaken by explaining the humorous
references it would be meaningless to you unless I did so:
    Soup: Vermigelli. (This is a jelly which is used in cases of lice
to smear all over the body and the seams of clothes.)
    Joints: Pigge com stuffe

Vegetables: Murphies or curlies

Sweets: Daillie news. (This was served out to all regiments from the News pudding fund cum out of bounds sauce.) All heavy intoxicants are banned hence this description of brandy sauce.

Beaunainville droppers. (You will remember that my very first letters from France all mentioned that apples were very plentiful. This was at Beaunainville.)

Canaries and Jamaicas. (Bananas)

W—s [deleted by censor]. (Red and white wines, malaga, citron, grenadine and whisky for officers and those desirous.) [27/12/15]

In 1916 the whole section was taken to an aerodrome some distance away for Christmas dinner provided by the Army with the officers present. They had a full turkey dinner followed by entertainment with Willie playing his violin. Then on Boxing Day another feast:

For several weeks I have been saving the tinned fruits you so kindly send me and they made part of our fourth course at dinner. We had soup, pork, apple sauce, sage and onion stuffing. Potatoes and turnips followed by plum pudding, brandy sauce and the fruit. Not bad eh? [26/12/16]

Christmas the following year, 1917, saw four of the boys saving up cash and food parcels for an extra celebration. They were fortunate enough to be billeted in the outhouse of an estaminet where they were normally fed from Army rations, occasionally supplemented by the landlady with soup, French bread and a nightly cup of delicious black coffee. They were served with the following meal on Christmas Eve, including a fresh chicken sent by relatives of Willie who lived in Worsthorne, a village just outside Burnley, which was to play an important part in his later life:

Our late dinner table at about 6.00 p.m. was graced by le petit poule from Worsthorne. It arrived in fine condition and Madame warmed it in the oven and improved it with onion sauce etc. Then we had the army issue of plum pudding and the other usual items of food, the whole washed down with Banyuls, a light port wine. Add to this our café noir and a cigar and you will realise that we felt very comfortable. [27/12/17]

They were still in the same billet a few weeks later and had a near repeat:

We were entertained to a late Sunday dinner. We had soup, chicken and chipped pommes de terre français, then paté and salad all washed down with vin rouge, café noir and cigars, so you will see that we occasionally click. [13/2/18]

At times the comrades were able to club together to pay a small supplement to a landlady. They were envious of some colleagues who had done even better:

Their good people regale them with rabbit and trout and maybe with woodcock and pheasant, washed down with real

*cider. I've had some, I know. In a more modest fashion our
own landlady is just as hospitable and kind. The few francs a
week which this costs is simply nominal and inadequately out
of all proportion to what we receive. [6/5/18]*

Willie had perhaps forgotten his own luck a couple of years
before when he was also billeted, with Cannon, in a French
house. They were so well looked after that they even referred
to their landlady as mother rather than Madame:

*Enclosed is a photograph of mother and her two children. She
was so good to us when I was with Cannon. She used to give
us coffee, salad and now and again eggs and other dainties.
She was, with all due respect, the nicest Belgian person I have
ever met out here. We were very sorry to leave what was
without doubt the best billet we have ever had. She was indeed
a mother to us. [28/7/16]*

One pitifully sad event concerning food, not recounted until
long after the war, occurred immediately after the Battle
of the Somme where casualties, dead and wounded, ran
to hundreds of thousands and the survivors were bogged
down in mud. The requisitions for food lagged well behind
the numbers of men left to feed with the result that twice
as much was reaching the forward positions as could be
consumed. The bully beef came in large tins about a foot
long and there was so much to spare that the men used the
unopened tins as cobble stones to make dry paths through the
mud.

A happier incident from the early days shows that sometimes a food bonus could arise in less tragic, and indeed amusing circumstances:

I am some distance due east of Boulogne. On Friday Woolfe and I drew rations for the section from a village about a mile and a half away where large quantities of meat, bread, jam, bacon, milk, cheese, butter, tea, sugar, salt etc. – also candles – were spread on tarpaulin at the roadside. It was very dark and misty and the lights of the motor lorry convoy proceeding along the road were combined with the noise of the horses and the swearing of most of the men. Some were swearing at the horses, some at the boxes of provisions, which they could not open because the tools had not arrived and most of them at one another, presumably to keep warm. Many mistakes occurred in the dark and we were fortunate to obtain many times our ration of butter. [19/9/15]

Bella Whittaker recounted to her grandsons, long after the war, that when Willie came home on leave she had got together all his favourite foods as treats on his brief visit. When the first meal back home was proffered he said that anything would do as he was so used to having to eat whatever was served, or available in the war zone. Of course he ate heartily and I am sure he enjoyed it doubly, sat at the family table before a roaring fire.

A nice passage from one letter serves as a suitable conclusion to this chapter and proves that whatever they may have had to put up with, at times Tommy fared pretty well, taking every advantage of extra food whenever off duty:

From Brouay to Servins, where we spent all our pay on food and lived like lords. A four course dinner every day. Soup, joint, pudding biscuits and cheese, tea and coffee. Not bad for Privates and on active service. [28/10/16]

All in all Tommy did not eat badly!

13

Tobacco and Alcohol

Cigarettes were smoked by almost all men in whatever walk of life or social class for most of the twentieth century and certainly until well after the Second World War. There were free issues to all the troops on active service in France, regarded at that time as absolutely necessary for morale and as a stress reliever. The writer, who served in the RAF in the Middle East during the Suez crisis in 1966, recalls that the French soldiers in the force which invaded Egypt were still being issued with a free weekly ration and the British forces in Cyprus could, and were encouraged to, buy blocks of 200 king-size cigarettes at the duty-free price of one shilling, or five pence in today's money, for twenty. The writer was the only man in his section of about 100 maintenance engineers who did not smoke!

How times have changed with the knowledge of the deadly medical consequences of long-term cigarette smoking – to the extent that a century after the outbreak of the First World War it is becoming socially unacceptable to smoke at all. It is arguable, however, whether, if this knowledge had been available in 1914, smoking would have been discouraged. The benefits of smoking may have outstripped any long-term health problems in the relief it brought in times of great physical danger.

It is obvious from the letters not only that all men smoked and that cigarettes were issued to every man, but that they were what today would be described as heavy smokers. Quite inadvertently Willie betrayed the rate of consumption when he wrote about a trip to the stores for the free tobacco ration:

We received three packets of twenty 'Three Witches' cigarettes each and an ounce of B.D.V. tobacco, which will keep us going for a day or two. [19/9/15]

This implied that at least thirty cigarettes a day would be smoked by each recipient and most of the men also had pipes, Willie certainly had one sent in a parcel from home, so the tobacco would also have been smoked. Add to this the inclusion of cigarettes in every parcel, of such long-forgotten brands as Gold Flake and Black Cat, not only sent by his parents – remembering that Tom Whittaker managed a tobacconist's shop in Burnley – but also occasionally from friends. Then there were local cigarettes bought very cheaply, so it is likely that average consumption was at least forty a day.

The availability of British cigarettes and the price of those bought locally were clearly of great importance, bearing in mind the very low pay of the private soldier and the addictive craving for tobacco:

You remember in my last letter I asked you not to send so much tinned fruit at present but instead add a few more cigarettes. The reason is that now having left Belgium, where English cigarettes were to be had at the old English price of threepence for ten I cannot get cigarettes for less than sixpence and now have to carry the infantry pack and equipment (excepting rifle and ammunition) so have had to reduce personal items to a minimum. [1/8/16]

I was pleased to receive your parcel including the splendid chicken and also the fine cigarettes, many thanks. I have also received the small parcel of Three Nuns cigarettes. By the way, our cigarette ration has been much better this last three weeks. We have had Lucana, B.D.V., and Crayd respectively. It is much better to get a few good cigarettes than a good many of mongrel brand. [9/12/16]

Willie was guarding German prisoners for a time in 1917 and observed that they would give anything for cigarettes:

Sergeant Dennis, Cannon and I are daily in charge of gangs of German prisoners performing elementary sanitary work, burying and burning refuse and generally clearing up. The prisoners are docile and on the whole work well. [22/12/17]

In the course of my work with the German prisoners it has been seen to me how necessary is tobacco to man. I have seen them trying to barter gold rings for a packet of cigarettes. [17/12/17]

One can only speculate that the reason for a request for extra cigarettes from home on one occasion might have been that Willie was himself engaging in a little barter:

Please send in future parcels a few more cigarettes than you have done previously. I cannot, unfortunately, give the reason for this request without committing a military offence. You may spend on cigarettes the money you have spent on tinned stuff. [28/7/16]

One of the saddest recollections that Willie recounted to his sons decades after the war featured the universal cigarette. He was walking along a trench after some heavy German shelling and came upon the gruesome sight of the headless corpse of a British Tommy with a cigarette clutched in his lifeless fingers. It was still alight, so the man can only have been dead for a few minutes.

Alcohol was a different matter. The men were forbidden to partake of 'heavy liquor', presumably meaning spirits in normal times. This seems strange considering that in the Navy a rum ration was issued free every day. Rum was only issued to soldiers when an offensive was planned. The only other time when alcohol was served free was on Christmas Day, when beer was provided with the traditional dinner and even whisky was available.

In one letter Willie recounts that the lads did not get their fair share on one occasion when rum was issued as it was intercepted by the sergeants en route and these worthies, predictably, took copious draughts before sending it on up the line.

There were Army-run canteens serving beer in many encampments and the local towns and villages also provided ample opportunity for Tommy to imbibe. Most of these remained more or less intact, but even in places which had been devastated by shelling, a semblance of normal life continued, and they all contained estaminets where off-duty troops could spend their pay on whatever was on offer. Beer and wine were the regular tipples, though it is hard to see how a ban on spirits could have been enforced there. Willie recounts buying Guinness at eight pence a bottle from the canteen and drinking one every night for a while.

The penalty for drunkenness was severe and Willie recounted one horrific example in an otherwise amusing tale of one Tree, a drunken driver:

Last night we went to the cinematograph entertainment provided by a divisional chaplain, which will now travel with the division. This pleasure was ours on the instigation of our officer, who not only gave us permission to go – it took place six miles away – but even paid admission for all and allowed the lorry to be used to take us there and bring us back. However, after the entertainment, we jumped back into the lorry and when we started discovered, by the erratic course which the lorry took, that something was very much wrong. By the fierce altercation which then ensued between our Staff Sergeant, who was riding in the front, and the driver, we learnt that the latter was very drunk. While we had been enjoying the pictures he had evidently been drinking very heavily in a nearby estaminet. The 'Staff' demanded that Tree leave the wheel and allow Marshall, the second driver, to take charge whereupon Tree threatened to run us into a ditch if the order was repeated. Staff said it again and, caring nothing,

Tree ran us into a ditch and almost overturned the lorry. Of course, we all dismounted and commenced what would be a very long walk: the time was then 9.00 p.m. Tree drove off and left us to it and a few minutes afterwards we fortunately met the bus which goes to meet the train at St Omer and we made it home very comfortably. Tree is now under arrest and is liable to any punishment from death to being tied to a cartwheel for many hours. We do not think he will receive a big punishment but most think he will get about six months. [4/11/16]

The sad tale of Tree was an exception as drunkenness was very rare, as was recalled after another entertainment in the form of a Charlie Chaplin film:

The chaplain called us to order and before singing 'God save the King' he informed us we should be able to get some good beer until half past eight at the canteen opposite which was open this extra half hour by special permission. How would that little incident go down with the prohibitionists? Before the war I bet the same parson would never have thought to advise fellows where to buy intoxicants. If war is having so broad an effect on parsons out here then let us encourage every member of the cloth to pay France a visit in wartime: it would do them good. If they were too narrow-minded to notice anything else they could not help seeing that a drunken Tommy in France is a rarity. [9/3/17]

Another drink-related incident was also rather amusing:

Quartermaster Keenan who was with us last night is one of the most entertaining fellows I have ever met. He is a true born Scot and has that fine sense of humour which one so often finds in a Scot. He is a Glasgow University man. He was telling us of one evening when he went into the Colonel's hut and saluted the bottle of whisky that was on the table. The Colonel did not take the hint however and he had to be content with a cup of coffee. He then explained that there are two kinds of Scots – one who 'taks' (takes) and one who 'gies' (gives) and they are called MacTaks and MacGees and the Colonel, says Keenan is a Mactak. [18/7/16]

A more compelling story about a Scot and alcohol was recounted by Willie long after the war. He met up with a Scottish regiment at one point and was chatting with a sergeant piper who had been awarded the Victoria Cross, the highest award for gallantry and given in only the most exceptional circumstances.

When asked about what act of extreme bravery he had performed the piper recounted that he had ascended the parapet of a captured trench while his comrades were advancing further under heavy fire. He started to play the bagpipes while marching up and down before the trench, with bullets whistling about him, and miraculously escaped unharmed. The returning troops, minus many fallen men, were full of praise for the heroic act, which had given them courage to capture more ground from the enemy.

The piper was then asked what it felt like to face death in this brave but foolhardy manner, whereupon he said that he had absolutely no recollection of the incident. 'You see,' he said, 'when we captured the German trench I discovered a full bottle of rum, I immediately drank a large amount of it and I remembered nothing for a few hours until I woke up in the trench.'

Willie recalled another amusing incident from when he was still in uniform and by now acting sergeant, after the war was over in 1919 but when he was still in France, very annoyed at the delay in demobilisation. He was in Boulogne, where he had met his old friend John Kippax, who was on his way home to be demobbed after his service in Salonica. They were in a café, when a grateful older French lady insisted on buying them the best drink in the house. They were served with 'rainbow cocktails', which consisted of layers of different coloured liqueurs of slightly varying specific gravity so that they did not mix unless stirred. The result was a multicoloured striped beverage of lethal power! After a couple of these the lady invited them to her home but, suspecting a possible hidden agenda, the two comrades had enough of their wits still about them to refuse. Perhaps they feared the penalty the Army might exact if such an escapade were discovered.

Willie and John were to marry sisters and became brothers-in-law as well as friends, and remained in close contact throughout their long marriages.

14

Entertaining the Troops

Whatever the shortcomings of the High Command in their military tactics, which history has demonstrated cost hundreds of thousands of lives quite needlessly, they had learnt many lessons from previous conflicts. The benefits of good health and hygiene and the contribution to morale, well-being and fitness made by proper feeding saw living conditions vastly better than ever before, miserable though life in the trenches could be.

The other enormous step forward in maintaining morale was that entertainment in the battle zone was well organised, with the arrangement of concert parties, often involving professional artists sent out from Britain, as well as the setting up of cinematographs in virtually every base camp to show films. The troupes from Blighty were supplemented by others made up of talented soldiers already serving in France and virtually every soldier, including front-line infantry, was able to attend. Some of the parties were set up by society ladies and even royalty! Audiences were typically 1,000 or more and some shows were put on within the range of enemy fire.

The concert parties always had a catchy name and included comedians, singers, instrumentalists, all male – sometimes impersonating females until 1919 when, with the war over, troupes including women were allowed to come from Britain.

The entertainments were by no means rare and the boys could certainly expect to see a live performance every couple of months:

Last night at the YMCA we had a splendid concert. Princess Victoria and Lena Ashwell arranged concert parties just after the war commenced to amuse Tommy. At first these concerts were confined to base towns and districts only but last night four gentlemen members of the Ashwell party came to this village and entertained us admirably. It is stated that this is the first time that a party of English civilians has been allowed so near the trenches. No ladies were allowed to come up however. We had a splendid cellist and a fine tenor and a more than usually good baritone. The very sight of their 'civvie' clothes was refreshing. The fourth member, who was in charge, was a raconteur and performer on the piano. The local soldiers are almost entirely from Lancs and Yorks regiments and the raconteur explained that he was born in Manchester, where he was a church organist. He then gave us a piece of dialect poetry entitled 'Come whoam to the childer and me'. [18/2/16]

I went to a concert last night – the Cheerio Boys were the performers and they were members of the division. We had a fine tenor, baritone, light comedian and low comedian and a piano and two violins, some show. It was all the more remarkable because it took place where the big — [censored

– but clearly the Battle of the Somme] commenced. Of course, all the jokes and funny bits were a trifle spicy and perhaps unsuitable for select entertainment but everyone enjoyed the show which was sufficient. The artists were rigged out in traditional pierrot style. [5/9/16]

There is a civilian theatre here which is now occupied by a troupe of soldiers called the Barn Owls. I went to hear their show last night and confess I expected to be bored but no; they gave a better show than I have often seen in a variety theatre at home. [21/9/16]

The Barn Owls were evidently at the local theatre for a season and as well as concerts like the above, they staged full revues for which there was a proper printed programme. The programme for an original musical revue called 'I Spy' was enclosed in another letter. The programme was priced one penny and was in three scenes: 'Interior of a house in London', 'At the foot of the cliffs', and 'On the cliffs'. Dresses were by courtesy of Miss Phyllis Dare and it must have been quite something to read the list of characters: Miss Smith, the governess; Lightning, a servant; Amelia Miller, the heroine; Lieutenant Bayswater R.N.; Jack Tar, his manservant; Fritz Krupt, a German spy; and Sherlock Blake, investigator.

All the actors were men and the revue featured choruses, songs and dances and ended with a ventriloquist sketch! The plot can almost be followed without being there with the obvious love interest thwarted for a time by the strict governess, the dastardly threat posed by the German spy and the successful unravelling of the mystery by the master detective. All would end well with the lovers in each other's arms and the German spy pushed off the cliff to his doom. The investigator bore the composite name of the two most popular fictional detectives of the time, Sherlock Holmes and Sexton Blake.

It was not certain that the German troops were given such thoughtful treatment. Conventional thinking suggests that their sense of duty was morale enough:

In this village a pianist group has commenced to perform. It is purely amateur, being composed of men of the 3rd Division, but although amateur it is a fine show. I wonder if the Germans have amusements behind their lines. [21/1/16]

The favourite concert party was The Snipers, a divisional pierrot group who performed right up to the front line, where Willie saw them in person, and were so good that they were sent to Blighty specially to perform for men back home. The most-loved member was a Northern comedian named Shackleton, who was from the Lancashire village of Trawden and known affectionately as 'Shack'.

I saw a performance by The Snipers last Friday and Shackleton told me that before crossing the channel they were to give a show in Boulogne. The party can truly claim to have performed on the firing line for last Friday's concert took place less than a mile from Fritz and I have see them perform nearer to the enemy line than they did last Friday. [21/3/17]

Just how dangerous it was to be putting on a show so near the enemy was tragically demonstrated by the news in a later letter that 'Shack' had been killed. Fortunately for posterity Willie described one of Shack's jokes, which always had the troops rolling in the aisles:

The best turn in The Snipers is the comedian from Trawden. I was speaking to him a few days ago and he seems to have been a sort of pub vocalist. He often topped the bill for Johnny Catlow's Market Tavern and has appeared at the Palace in Burnley more than once. He was a really clever comedian and although he often tells his yarns in the broadest dialect and the majority of the audience are southerners he is always encored. He told a story about a West Country constituency electing the squire, Sir George, as Member of Parliament. When the poll had been declared, the new M.P. gave a speech in which he particularly praised farmer Steer for his help as a canvasser. Twelve months later, farmer Steer, who happened to be visiting a cattle market in the vicinity, went to Sir George's house in Park Lane London. He rang the bell and the butler carried his name to Sir George who said 'humph, most unfortunate, we're just about to have dinnah however, show him to the armchair by the fire and I will chat to him during dinnah.' Farmer Steer was safely seated and the following conversation ensued:

Sir George: Good day farmer Steer and how are you?

Steer: Oi be orlright Sir George.

Sir George: And how are things at the farm pray?

Steer: They be none too bad. The old zow she have had a litter of 13 – and 13 be an unlucky number zur.

Sir George: Why unlucky pray?

Steer: Well, you see, the old zow she has nobbut 12 tits.
(At this juncture the females rattled their plates and endeavoured
to change the conversation)

Sir George: And what happened to poor little number 13?

Steer: Well you see zur. He have to sit on his bum and watch
t'other pigs feed like I be doing now.

It was uproariously enjoyed. [17/1/17]

Another joke, from the comedian in The Very Lights, was reported just a few days later, demonstrating that concert parties visited frequently:

A butcher's boy got into a railway carriage carrying the usual
pastry cook's basket. At the next station a portly old gentleman
entered the carriage and sat immediately under the basket. At
intervals he pulled out his handkerchief and vigorously wiped
the back of his neck. At last, in great anger, he leaned over
the small youth and, slapping him on the knee, said loudly
'Do you know young rascal that the gravy from your pies is
running down my neck?' 'Pies' said the boy 'Them's not pies,
them's pigs.' [28/3/17]

In Willie's opinion, the best concert party was The Fancies:

The violinist was wonderful. It cost me 3d to hear him. I don't
think you would be able to hear the same class of performance
in England for under about two shillings. There was a comedian
who very ably imitated Willie Bard, George Roby, Albert

Whelan, and George Formby frae Lancaster. He gave an original patter after Formby's cigarette business style: 'there's not one you couldn't get three of four draws out on'. After telling you about the cigarettes he put them in different pockets. In one instance he put two cigs into the same pocket but drew one back with the remark: 'Ah, nearly made a mistake then – NCOs going in wi officers'. Then there was a real Jewish comedian who sang about Sgt Isaac Solomon, the very first yiddisher Scotsman in the Irish Fusiliers. Then there was a splendid 'girl', a tenor, baritone and a fine solo pianist, all of them splendidly costumed and accompanied by an orchestra of about twenty performers. Tonight, The Whizzbangs are performing but they cannot compare with The Fancies. [2/4/17]

George 'frae Lancaster' was George Formby senior, whose son, George junior, was to be one of the greatest entertainers of the Second World War. Yet another concert party, The Dumbells, also had a good comedian, who gave a biblical parody of the Canadian forces going into the Battle of the Somme:

On the third day the tribe of Canadia came unto a village in Somaria (Somme Area) and rested. The village had many inns and on that night the fighting men partook freely the vintage thereof. And in the darkness they were taken into their sleeping quarters and when they saw them they murmured amongst themselves saying 'here is a hole which once was not bad but now is.' and another sayeth, pointing to the sky, here is once a roof which is no more.' And they became exceeding wrath. Then they said 'Oh chieftain what shall we eat?' and the chieftain distributed amongst them the flesh of oxen (bully) and they ate. And on the morrow after the plague (lice) had caused them great torment they girded on their wherewithal and marched forward. [8/10/17]

Even after the war was over the concert parties kept coming. Of course, demobilisation was very slow and many troops remained in France throughout 1919:

Last night I spent a very enjoyable evening at the Armand Pavillion, a concert group of about nine performers. The Nightingales ambitiously attempted 'Dick Whittington' and succeeded remarkably well. The costumes were splendid, including that of the cat. The performance was made all the more novel by making Dick and the rest of the cast join up in the army and come to France, where the dame and fair Alice were both WAACS. [19/1/19]

At this time French theatrical troupes had also emerged, no doubt cashing in on full audiences of Tommies, paying a few pence each but making a reasonable total sum:

Last night I enjoyed a French concert group in the Pavilion. It is a good number of years since I have enjoyed hearing such talented artists and particularly the tenor, the violinist, cellist and pianist. It was gorgeous. [18/2/19]

Even the Americans provided entertainment after they came into the war:

I enjoyed an impromptu concert in an estaminet in F— last night. Three or four coal black Negroes made melody, classical and otherwise. [16/10/18]

There were plenty of silent movies for the soldiers to watch, Charlie Chaplin being a popular favourite. The cinemas were often a part of a YMCA set-up and one or two enterprising chaplains also arranged shows:

We have a cinema here, where there is a change of performance nearly every night so you will realise that our evenings need not be dull. [7/6/16]

The other evening we visited the cinema, which is always packed full, where Charlie Chaplin provided a pleasant diversion from the humdrum and nerve-racking life of the firing line. Many of the men had to go straight after the performance to buckle on their packs and proceed to the trenches as working parties. The regiments that are out of the line send a small party of men to the trenches each night to repair the trenches themselves, mend barbed wire, dugouts and so forth and also to carry up ammunition and food. [18/6/16]

Another form of entertainment came from the regimental bands, which often gave concerts as well as carrying out their normal military duties:

A good band also amused us with William Tell and other old favourites. Have you ever thought about the important part played by bands in this war? They make the marches easier for one thing. Here is another instance of their value. A certain band used to practice daily at a place, Ph—, about fourteen miles from Fritz. I have myself stood in our front line in front of Ph— and heard the strains of the band carried to us on the breeze. The point is that the breeze also carried the melody over to Fritz and gave him strong evidence of the cheerful spirit which exists on this side. The band always made a point of playing various allied national songs at the end of the show. This must be very galling to the enemy. [8/10/17]

There is a divisional theatre at this place and during the past three weeks we have enjoyed several concerts there. The divisional band performs there once or twice a week and you will understand the pleasure I derive from their efforts. One of my acquaintances, Sgt Symonds of The Buffs, performs therein. At present he is playing the violin in a full brass band! But this is pro tem and when his other instrument arrives from England he will be playing the saxophone. [11/10/16]

The efforts of a French military band were also noted:

An hour or so ago the band of a certain famous French regiment was playing just before our billet. The music was martial but in some inexplicable way it was very different from our English music of similar character. Another unusual feature was that the music was rendered conjointly by two different bands each with its own conductor. One band, composed of the usual military band instruments, formed up in the customary circle and I counted thirty six performers. About ten yards away there was a bugle band of twenty four men composed of sixteen ordinary bugles and eight small French horns. Throughout the performance the band played bugle calls which synchronised perfectly with the more intricate pieces being played by the large band. [6/5/18]

The troops also designed their own entertainment and at one period Willie was secretary of a sectional football team, arranging fixtures and venues:

We have arranged a football club and are doing the thing in style by getting jerseys etc. Although pressed, I have refused to play, realising that with football one is very susceptible to colds etc. but I am able to take part in club affairs by performing the secretarial duties. [23/10/17]

I assure you that our football club is being carried on with all seriousness and the committee meetings are treated sincerely. The trouble with my secretaryship is that I have not sufficient authority to arrange dates of matches as I would wish. [5/11/17]

Our first two matches have produced rather funny results. In the first, on an away ground, we were beaten 7-1 whilst in the second, on our own ground, we won 8-0. We are to play another sanitary section on Friday, when excitement will prevail. [12/5/17]

The football came to an untimely end, however, when a local farmer, doubtless the owner of the land, intervened:

The other afternoon we played the 62nd sanitary section on our own ground. The result was a 1-1 draw. A pleasant convivial evening followed, with story and music to pass the time. I will now tell you a little incident which occurred before the match. Our home ground was on a fairly level piece of land but pitted with shell holes. All our spare time for about a fortnight had been absorbed in filling in these depressions and obliterating the consequent mounds where earth had been thrown up. We also marked the field with dazzling whiteness and the day before the match the ground was a credit and delight to all of us. Imagine our dismay when at 2 o'clock on the afternoon of the match we walked to the ground and found a French farmer in full possession of the ground busily ploughing it! There were many angry murmurs – blankety-blank, dash etc. However, we struck a hockey pitch, with small goals, and played there. [19/11/17]

Then there were games. The section owned a chess set and of course packs of cards. The usual card game was 'Nap', a favourite wherever Tommy was located. This was a simple form of whist, involving only five cards per player with each player bidding to take a number of tricks, the highest bid winning the right to name the trump suit. To bid all five was called 'going nap', and this phrase is still used to designate the number five – especially if a soccer team scores five goals or a cricket bowler takes five wickets. It is probable that most twenty-first-century journalists using the expression have no idea of its origin! Nap was a good gambling game as it was mostly a question of luck, but had an edge of skill which would bring the better player on top after several games.

Sometimes there was even the possibility of normal civilian recreation. In the early days in France, Willie and some comrades went boating, courtesy of the gardener of a large chateau:

France. We are beautifully situated here in a little country cottage in a nice part of north —. The district here is all intersected with canals and waterways and through the agency of one of my pals (Phillips), who can speak French well, we are able to borrow a light skiff, fishing tackle etc. and we have had one or two fine expeditions on the water. [20/5/15]

Then there was some swimming at one period when they were working at base headquarters:

I am back at HQ, situated near a small French town and amidst lovely country. Our workshop, billet etc. are in what before the war was a sort of village concert hall. From the window the ground slopes down to our bathing pool. At this very moment Kilburn is on the springboard and Black and one or two others are making a merry splash. It is a refreshing sight and when this letter is finished I shall go in for a swim 'tout de suite'. [21/7/18]

I am writing this in our cosy little writing room overlooking the swimming pool where just over an hour ago I was enjoying a lovely dip which has produced splendid freshness and coolness. [2/8/18]

Hobbies provided further diversions. Willie had his violin-playing and for all there was reading, discussion among themselves – often of a serious nature – and writing letters home. It is interesting to see from the letters that Willie read the newspapers and magazine articles regularly sent by his parents, but most of his literature was in the form of books by classic authors such as Shakespeare, Shaw and Oscar Wilde plus serious writing by contemporary pedagogues such as Horatio Bottomley:

I would be obliged if you could send a copy of G. B. Shaw's book An Unusual Socialist. *There are some pretty stiff statements in it and they could perhaps come in useful in promoting discussion. It is a good way of passing the dull evenings to have arguments, which will perhaps be instructive. Please also send Oscar Wilde's* A picture of Dorian Gray *which Cannon strongly recommends to me. [31/10/15]*

Willie was also anxious to improve his education and had his parents send him English grammar and arithmetic text books as well as primers in the French language. The letters show that he worked diligently at these, determined to give himself a better chance in the post-war job market.

The boys in the section were always ready for a leg-pull or a practical joke, which must also have helped to pass the time. One rather cruel example was described:

We had a rather amusing time in the billet last night. Phillips, while out with the section dog, Jim, found a hedgehog and brought it back to camp. It is customary for the boys to make beds before going out – you perhaps know that on rising blankets must be folded and stacked at the head of the bed. Phillips decided to give 'Nigger' Woolfe a bed companion and put the hedgehog into the bed. Nigger undressed, pushed his feet beneath the blankets and —! [16/10/16].

Soldiers in the First World War were famous for their songs. They alleviated the drudgery of marching, and there was a touch of nostalgia or even homesickness in the most famous of them, such as 'Take me back to dear old Blighty, set me down in old London town, give me time to spare. Take me anywhere, Liverpool, Leeds or Birmingham, I don't care', 'Pack up your troubles in your old kit bag and smile, smile, smile', or 'It's a long way to Tipperary, it's a long way to go'.

Willie reported the singing of several ditties – one about the weekly magazine *John Bull*, which survived into the 1950s, cynically parodying the optimism of Horatio Bottomley, who had forecast an early end to the war:

> *If it is in John Bull it is so, it is so.*
> *We know Horatio never was a fool*
> *So I always keep these copies by*
> *And that's why I can prophesy*
> *That the war was over in July*
> *For it said so in John Bull. [19/11/17]*

Another was sung to the tune of 'Yes Jesus Loves Me':

> *Lord Kitchener loves us*
> *Yes, Kitchener loves us*
> *Yes, Kitchener loves us*
> *And so he bally well ought.*

We can be certain that 'bally' was not the actual word used!

Perhaps a song from one of the shows by Willie's favourite concert party, sums up the attitude and also the sentiments of soldiers serving in foreign field:

The latest popular song, popularised by The Fancies, is just the sort of ditty to please Tommy:

> *Blighty, Blighty, that's the place we're going back to.*
> *Blighty, Blighty, mother put my nightie by the fire to air.*
> *I'll be there*
> *Hear those bells a ringing, hear those Tommies singing*
> *Blighty, Blighty, hear those big propellers making music in the foam.*
> *See that transport ready to start*
> *See that transport keen to depart*
> *What! You don't know where Blighty is?*
> *Why – bless your heart – it is the soldiers' home sweet home.*

The concert party comedians are in the enviable position of being able to get a bit of their own back on the officers and Sergeant Majors etc. Last night one gave a little rhyme which mercilessly made fun of Generals, to the great enjoyment of Tommy. I noticed that one of the Generals present laughed just as heartily as the rest of us. Generals are evidently human after all. [10/7/17]

The sustained loyalty to king and country, in spite of the horrendous slaughter, is difficult to comprehend through twenty-first-century eyes. The following occurred only a few months after the Battle of the Somme:

After the band concert the other night, when 'The King' was played, I looked round at everybody standing to attention and wondered if, after the war, we shall see people filing out of theatres while it is being played. Personally I think that for many years at least people will remain still until the end of the national anthem. It is a little way of showing that we love our country. [11/10/16]

The playing of the national anthem after film shows was adopted as standard practice in cinemas after the war and indeed this practice continued until after the Second World War. The audience stood to attention. Greater social freedom and possibly less respect for the monarchy soon resulted in people moving to the exits before the end of the music. For a brief period cinemas tried playing only the first three lines but even this had to be abandoned. In a rather oblique way, this surely demonstrated that it was no longer the case that men would, without question, face death on the battlefield rather than risk dishonour.

15

Music, Music, Music

The varied and regular entertainment provided by the authorities was without doubt a major factor in maintaining morale among the troops on active service. In the previous chapter we have seen how film shows were provided and concert parties visited at frequent intervals. Some of the more talented men themselves also provided entertainment for their comrades and although there were times of boredom, in the trenches themselves or in the billets on dull evenings, Tommy always had recent entertainment to recall or something to look forward to soon.

William Whittaker was a very good violinist. He had been encouraged to learn the instrument as a boy by his uncle Jim in Burnley and studied under a great Northern teacher, Albert Pollard. He played duets as a teenager with his close friend Harry Preston. The story of their estrangement and reconciliation has already been recounted.

Quite soon after his arrival in the war zone, Willie firstly borrowed a violin and then had one sent out by his parents:

A Sergeant from a unit billeted in the same cottages as us had been on leave and brought a violin back. He kindly lent it to me one afternoon and I enjoyed playing 'Intermezzo' and one or two others. I could pass many a dull hour out here with a violin and a Star *album. [11/1/16]*

The *Star* albums were collections of favourite pieces for violin with piano accompaniment. He played regularly throughout his four years in France, to the delight of his comrades. Music was sent from home together with accessories such as new strings when required. A new bottom string, the G, would have cost about 3 pence in today's money. As an illustration of inflation, such a string of average quality might now cost £10.00.

I have about an hour's practice every night on the violin, which reminds me that the G string is broken. I have pieced it up once or twice but it has now broken so much that I cannot possibly use it again so please send me another and don't spend more than 8d *on it. [9/11/16]*

Luckily for Willie, one of the senior NCOs in his section also played the instrument so there was a sympathetic environment and there were many impromptu performances in the billets. The influence of this sergeant meant that violin and music were transported from place to place as official baggage. Otherwise it would have been impossible for a private to carry them around:

Sergeant Gooding, who is a violinist, is now our acting Staff Sergeant and several weeks ago he urged me to get my fiddle sent out. Consequently it will be up to him to see that it is carried about when we move. [11/10/16]

At the Christmas party we had a piano from the cinema and enjoyed beaucoup de music and fun. Sergeant Gooding was unfortunately out of condition so the whole of the violin playing fell on me. I played 'Melody in F', 'L'abeille', and Il Trovatore *and I think the last was performed a little after my old style. [26/2/16]*

The most rewarding musical experiences he had was when he was welcomed into French families where there was a pianist. One family welcomed him regularly for some months before the section was moved away:

I am getting a lot of practice on the violin. Two or three times a week I visit the civilians and enjoy something like the old times. I have arranged for the transport of any music I might have so please send me, as soon as is convenient, 'Intermezzo' from Cavaleira Rusticana, *'Number one'* Star *album and the Singelée book including 'Der Pirat'. [1/1/17]*

I have spent a few evenings recently at the civilians' home and have enjoyed each better than the previous one. My pianist friend is just getting into the swing of Der Pirat *and* Barber of Seville *and in fact all the old pieces which were enjoyed so much in the dear old times. I have also got a selection from the* Cloches de Cornville *and it is very popular with the civilian friends who speak of the performance of this piece which they witnessed some time ago in France. [31/1/17]*

I was down at the civilians last Sunday and had a very enjoyable evening. There is a blind girl, a friend of theirs, who is a remarkable pianist and, after hearing me play Il Trovatore *the other night, she sat down and played it on the piano, in proper sequence and with very little error. It was astonishing. [14/3/17]*

With my violin I gained entrance to a civilian's house where I enjoyed good practice with the assistance of a pianist and a cellist. [1/9/17]

Willie had taken an opportunity which presented itself during a work visit to introduce himself to this new family and to enjoy the comfort of their fine house:

In the course of my duties I have been obliged to visit most of the houses in the village. I have had to make use of my best French to explain my business to the French civilian occupants and have commenced by wishing them good morning, 'bon jour'. I went to one big house and to my salutation the madame answered without any accent 'Good morning, come inside out of the rain and let me know what you require'. After recovering from the shock of hearing such good English from a civilian I explained my presence there and in the course of this I discovered that she was an Englishwoman. Whilst performing my work there, which had to do with the water, she spoke learnedly about the geological strata of the district and its effect on agriculture etc. I would have enjoyed staying a long time but I was busy and must needs depart. Passing through the house again I noticed a fine piano, littered on top with English songs, but could not on so short acquaintance and with regard to her standing, ask for an entry into her house for musical reasons but I hope to visit the house again and by a little tact and diplomacy I shall strike a musical note, figuratively, and may work the oracle. [15/1/18]

It is interesting to note the class awareness in the above comments. The lady was obviously a cut above a humble private soldier but all turned out well. The house turned out to be the home of a prosperous mill owner and it did not take Willie long to 'work the oracle', for shortly afterwards he was enjoying musical evenings with his violin and the very fine piano:

I had a fine musical evening last night at the home of the mill owner. He is evidently well off and the nice piano, good music and fine salon furniture made a pleasant change. [11/3/18]

With regard to the mill owner's house I spent one very enjoyable evening there and was treated most hospitably. A good piano and a good pianist (Sergeant Dennis, who has since left the district), my violin and the good people made a notably bright evening among the dull ones we have in France. [1/4/18]

The Belgian composer J. B. Singelée was a particular favourite. He specialised in operatic arrangements – pastiches of the best music from individual operas in the form of themes and spectacular variations which often required virtuoso skills. There was a vast collection of these works including most of the operas of Verdi (including *Il Trovatore*), Bellini (including *Der Pirat*), Rossini (including *Barber of Seville*). Puccini, Donizetti, Gounod and many lesser names. This kind of music was very popular at the time as staged opera was virtually inaccessible to any but wealthy city dwellers. The sheet music of the collection is still in the hands of the writer, also a violinist, who used to play them with his elder brother John, who was a good pianist. John had kept our father's letters for decades.

Willie entertained his fellows in many ways:

I shall be in a position in a few days time to visit my musical friends and to enjoy one of those evenings which were so pleasant a short time ago. I am also in touch with my pianist friend and hope to be able to have a few good times with him. From time to time I have played at the cinema and have enjoyed this practice very much. [9/3/17]

Talking films had not yet been invented and the tins containing the large reels of celluloid on which the films were reproduced came with a musical score fully marked up as to when and how the instrumentalists should play along with what was happening on the screen.

A spell at base saw Willie's talents in particular demand:

I am at HQ and hope to stay there for some time, although that is very unlikely. We have now got a piano for which we are to pay ten francs a month hire. The Sergeant Major goes

*on leave tonight and is to get some music – 'Salut d'amour',
'Humoresque', 'Melodie' by Thomé and some popular stuff.
[23/10/17]*

*I shall have to finish here tonight. A Sergeant from the chateau
next door has just been in and extracted my promise to go
down with the violin at 7 o'clock. It is 6.30 now and I must
wash and clean up. So long. [28/1/17]*

*It is really getting cold now and I must take myself below to
satisfy the persistent calls for 'Whitt' to perform on the violin
and gather the heat of a good fire unto myself. [28/10/17]*

*Sergeant Dennis, Cannon and I played at a concert the other
night. I played from memory the 'Simple Aveu' and was well
received so gave as an encore, by request, 'Humoresque'.
[20/12/17]*

Willie's fame was such that he and his pianist chum Cannon
were singled out for a special trip at Christmas to perform
at a Royal Flying Corps base some distance away from
HQ:

*The RFC sent a car for us two and I was rather chary of
exercising what some people are kind enough to call my musical
talents. At the concert which followed our turkey dinner at
the request of many of the men, whom I was among for the
first time, I played 'Humoresque', then 'Salut d'amour', 'Ave
Maria', 'Simple Aveu', Il Trovatore, 'Der Pirat', 'Intermezzo',*

'Rosary', *all from memory, and then about half a dozen more from the Star albums. It was only by promising to give them more music at some other time that the C.O. allowed us to depart at 2.00 a.m. (in a car) after taking a wee deoch & doris of Jamesons to keep out the cold. Snow had fallen to at least a couple of feet in depth. I mention this to show that the tot of Irish whiskey was necessary for health reasons. [27/12/17]*

Among the pieces always encored on these occasions was a little work called 'Simple Aveu' by the French composer Ambrose Thomas. The sheet music is still in use today!

As a result of the success of Willie's concerts, it was recommended that he join one of the divisional concert parties which supplemented the hugely popular visiting professional outfits. The one he nearly joined was made up of serving men and was called The Archies:

This morning our officer asked Sergeant Dennis if he and I were willing to assist the Corps concert party. We were agreeable and await developments with interest. Of course, little may come of it but on the other hand it may alter the whole course of our life in France. [28/11/17]

Unfortunately he was posted away from HQ and so nothing came of what would have been a great job. There was another opportunity of this kind a few months later after he had been in convalescent camp with a dose of 'flu', but his competence at his day job cost him the chance, though at least his recall led to his promotion to full corporal.

Well, I am back in the section at St Amand. The officer wrote specifically for my return to the section and it is due to his efforts that I am back so quickly. I was in hospital at 'con' camp at Étaples and had it not been that the war is over I could and should have stayed there at least three months as a violinist in one of the many orchestras performing in that district. [18/2/18]

The exigencies of Army life made it impossible for Willie to practice his instrument, or perform, all the time:

During the past six weeks I have had little opportunity for practice, it being almost impossible to carry a violin about when one never knows with what little warning he may have to fold his tents like the Arabs and steal away. In the army one can never tell how long he will rest in one place before he must take up his bed and walk (or ride if he is lucky). [8/1/17]

Because of the demobilisation rules but also because of his general competence and reliability, Willie, much to his displeasure, had to stay on in France for some eight months after the Armistice. The officer regarded him so highly that he was awarded a third stripe with the position of Orderly Room Sergeant. There his assistant was Bradley, his long-time comrade in the section. His new rank and duties must have made a big difference to his lifestyle and although he had by now sold his violin for fifty francs in anticipation of an early demob, which never seemed to come, there were more opportunities to enjoy music-making:

There have been several dances held in the town recently by the outgoing troops. They have been private 'dos', batteries, companies, regiments having their own affairs. I, of course, managed to get in when I could not resist the diversion offered by borrowing the violin I sold and making one in the band. [15/3/19]

More informal was work in a local bar-café and two weeks later in a hotel:

Several times during the week I have been pleased to perform on the violin in a Bethune estaminet to the intense gratification of the proprietess. Her daughter plays the piano remarkably well and in addition puts me to shame when she handles the violin. [5/7/19]

Then we had another walk around Lille and, returning to the 'Place', entered the most imposing hotel in the vicinity. Chairs and tables, shaded by plants and glass screens overflowed from the building proper onto the pavement outside. Inside was a blaze of electric light and a small orchestra of about eight players performed pleasantly in a corner of the large room. Under pressure from Bradley and with, I think, not a little encouragement from the good wine which coursed pleasantly through my veins, I asked for and received permission from the chef d'hotel to give a violin solo. I played the Intermezzo sufficiently well to retain my place with the orchestra for over an hour during which time I played as solos 'Melody in F' and 'Spring Song'. I played from memory, I may add. [22/7/19]

When he was demobbed, Willie inherited a nice instrument from his uncle Jim and as well as his regular job in the bank, he played professionally in the evenings at a local picture palace, the Tivoli in Burnley. There were still no talking pictures in the 1920s and the films always came with a musical score for a small band, minimally piano, violin and drums to liven up the action on the screen. He saved up for his marriage out of his earnings at the cinema.

Willie's wife Nellie was an accomplished pianist and the family home was always full of music-making. Willie also played regularly in local groups. He became leader of the Bingley orchestra for a time and then for thirty years was leader of the amateur symphony orchestra in Colne, Lancashire. He also played in the pit for various amateur operatic societies in their performances of musical comedy and operetta and remained in demand to play at church fetes for as long as he was physically able.

What a privilege it was to have such a stimulating hobby and how proud he must have been to be able to give so much joy to his comrades during his active service.

16

People and Language

Most ordinary Tommies would have no knowledge of the French language and even fewer would have ever left the shores of Britain. It must have been a double shock therefore to come into contact not only with a foreign language but an alien culture as well. Most of the time they were in any case only among their comrades, but when they were not actually in the trenches – and even the infantry spent more time behind the lines in support than actually in the very front line – they had to learn to cope with life in the local towns and villages, where life went on with a surprising degree of normality.

They soon learnt essential words like '*bière*' and '*vin*' for use in the estaminets and naturally would use '*bon jour*' to greet French people from the day they arrived. A sort of French argot crept into everyday language, so that for example '*Ça ne fait rien*' – translated as 'It doesn't matter' – became 'Sanfairian', a word which existed in military slang long after the Second World War! Opportunities to communicate in French were limited by simple lack of exposure to the natives. There were not even French troops to talk to as the British sector exclusively covered the north-east while the French Army was positioned at the front further south.

The better-educated troops, certainly the officers, who would all have studied French for many years at school, must have been able to get by pretty well and among the other ranks the minority who had been to grammar school knew some of the language.

The officers, who probably hardly needed it, had access to educational material, but it is very strange that there was no provision for language instruction for other ranks serving in France itself. There was not even an issue of phrase books let alone text books and formal teaching even for those willing to learn. There were French classes in London, run by society ladies for new recruits, but few attended them and even some of those were probably more interested in the free cakes and tea which were provided than a genuine curiosity about the French language.

William Whittaker was a grammar-school boy and, though leaving school at the age of fourteen, as was normal for all but the highly academic, he had been taught French for three years and was even congratulated on his pronunciation at the London classes. He was a very intelligent boy and his letters show that throughout his time in the Army he was constantly questing for knowledge. He read widely and he regularly requested quality literature from home, and as well as classical and contemporary material, he also asked for text books, naturally including French primers. He recounted his progress through the various chapters in his communications with his parents.

From the earliest days at the front, the letters contain French words and phrases used, without translation, to substitute the equivalent English. His father Tom Whittaker, in spite of his relatively humble origins, did understand French, and shortly after his son went abroad was actually teaching some basic French to potential recruits in Burnley.

I was surprised to read of your new role as a French master. [9/11/15]

The use of French words in correspondence is typically shown in this extract:

Corporal Black, Marfleet and I are billeted together a few miles from the remainder of the section and although very near to Fritz we are cosy and comfortable from an active service standpoint, if the floor is rather hard for an angular person like myself. Ah well, 'c'est la guerre' (this phrase is very popular with Tommy and is taking the place of 'Ça ne fait rien' in the soldier's collection of phrases). [9/3/17]

Soon after his arrival in France, Willie was finding his way in the language and sounded quite hopeful of mastering it:

The people's French is generally very clear and I am learning and gaining confidence in speech. [19//9/15]

Disillusionment soon set in however, and he became despondent about ever coming to grips with the language.

I feel so horribly ignorant of the French Language. There is really amazingly little opportunity of learning French which you will understand when I state that there must be about fifty thousand English against a few hundred natives near us. [9/11/15]

Your question about language is readily understood. Now and then I ambitiously set out to tell the locals something and, after racking my brains for some word or words I ought to know and failing in the attempt, I simply say 'Ça ne fait rien' and so close the conversation. You will never realise how useful signs and actions are until you find yourself among foreigners, knowing little of their language. Moreover we go to the civilians to play music which is fortunately printed in a universal language. [7/1/16]

When first sent to serve in Flanders Willie was in for a rude linguistic shock:

The language spoken around here is simply awful. French is musical compared to it, Flemish I think it is. [1/10/15]

Flemish it certainly was and like its companion language, Dutch, it is full of harsh, guttural sounds. No wonder that Willie, with his musician's ear, found it quite grating. That learning each other's language is a two-way process was charmingly described in a recollection a year after the event:

We arrived in Steenworde, we were in Flanders, the name of the town was sufficient to prove that. I remember meeting there a very pretty Belgian girl of about fourteen who spoke wonderful English. Her pronunciation was remarkable and she said that she knew no English word before Tommy appeared. Some youngster! [29/10/16]

Most of his service was in north-east France, close to the Belgian border, and Willie eventually became a fluent French speaker. By 1918 his command of the language was so good that he asked his father to send him an advanced grammar and material for him to read in French:

Thanks, Hugo's French Verbs *is to hand and appreciated. Could you send in some future parcel a few of* Hugo's French Journals *which I think you have knocking about somewhere. [7/7/18]*

In spite of having to learn the hard way, Willie was eventually in such command of the language that he even thought in French when in the company of natives. His ability was very useful when he went into French homes, as the sanitary engineers sometimes had to do house to house calls to check the water supply and drainage arrangements. His musical evenings off duty in civilian homes gave him another opportunity to improve his skills although at first the only common language was music. He also recounted amusing incidents translating for baffled American soldiers who served in France towards the end of the war and could not even buy refreshments in the local estaminets where the barmaids could not understand their unusual accents.

Although most of the section picked up reasonable French, not all were as proficient as Willie and had to resort to a phrase book. Woolfe had an interesting, and to the rest of the boys hilarious, experience:

A very amusing incident took place the other day. Woolfe, whose French is not quite 'par excellence', was carrying on a conversation with a French girl. He was using a phrase book and when he came away we asked him how he had progressed. 'Fine' says he. On enquiry we found that he had used only one phrase from the book which was 'The steamer is in sight'. The rest of the conversation was chiefly 'ah oui'. There must be hundreds of incidents of this type happening every day.

I think after the war French phrases and words will become quite common. For instance yesterday I was in the nearby estaminet and noticed how French cropped up in some conversations between Tommies such as 'Our leave has been stopped for six weeks comprenez?' and 'It's been a bon day hasn't it?' said in all seriousness. [7/12/15]

The letters contain as much social history as military and political history and make many interesting references to the culture of civilian France into which the troops had been thrown. Willie was a keen observer and in general the local inhabitants, at least on the Allied side of the line, did not let the war alter their traditional way of living very much:

The people of Beaunonville were very little affected by the war. I mean financially. They were all farmers and lived off and by the land and mother earth in war and peace. War does not change the way of producing a crop of potatoes, wheat or apples. [29/10/16]

The lighting regulations in Blighty seem to be very strict according to your letters and the newspapers. This is very remarkable to us out here for it would astonish you if you saw some of the lights which are exposed in these villages which are so close to the front line. Some of the shops have full lights in their windows and the windows are facing the front. You must not imagine that the villages are ablaze with light. There are no street lights at all and there are not many shops but familiarity breeds contempt and it is a fact that the danger seems to be scarcely recognised by the civilians. [23/11/16]

A somewhat cynical and ultimately cryptic analysis of civilian nonchalance followed a few months later:

We are not very far from the line here and the presence of civilians makes one think a little. There seem to be three reasons why they still endanger their lives by remaining in the area of the shelling. Firstly they may have a sentimental attachment to their old homes and districts, which no doubt weighs a lot with some people. Secondly, their reasons for living in such proximity to the line may be nothing more or less than greed. There are plenty of soldiers about, competition is not very strong and it is possible to sell goods to them at a greater profit than if they were outside the danger zone. The third reason for them living not far from Fritz I will leave you to guess at. [17/3/17]

There must have been civilian casualties as many towns and villages were flattened by German shelling – the same applying to habitations on the German side of the line shelled by the British – but Willie was nevertheless able to paint an almost idyllic rural pastoral scene in stark contrast to the horror of the front line:

Yesterday afternoon I toiled up to the very top of a slag heap from which a most wonderful view can be obtained. It is very high and the field and ground below looked like a patchwork quilt. I looked towards the front line, everywhere it was afire. Then I turned right around and looked in the other direction; chimneys all smoking, trains running and as little specks I could see the farmers working in their fields. What a difference! That line is burning to save what lies behind from a similar fate; oh dreadful, cruel, cleansing war. [23/4/17]

As France was a devout Roman Catholic country, the natives could not allow a transient thing like the war to interfere with their religious feasts, ceremonies and devotions. The public processions on holy days were evidently celebrated in all their demonstrative normality. In his typically deft style, and with a touch of his innate cynicism, Willie painted a colourful scene on one such occasion:

This afternoon, being the first Sunday in June, we have seen the Catholic church procession of the 'Sacré coeur'. Even in this small village it was made sufficiently spectacular and interesting to deserve a few lines. The road from the church door had been strewn with freshly cut grass and thousands of fine flowers, which made still more pleasant the blossom-scented air of the countryside. All the girls of course were dressed in white (the emblem of purity explained an army interpreter standing by). Whatever rights some of the females had to an emblem of purity I am not going to discuss for, if nothing else, white looks nice and was certainly in keeping with the occasion. At any rate they processed. At the head of the procession was the French tricolour which, as it passed by, was saluted by many British troops along the road – a pleasing incident! Then followed the usual banners of St Peter and St Paul and a host of others, each bearing the letters P.P.N. or in full 'Priere pour nous'. One gets used to seeing that phrase out here for every wayside shrine and every gravestone bears it – a prayer for us. After this part of the cortege came the priest, resplendent in his crown of gold and bearing in his arms a massive gilt ornament. He walked along under a gorgeous canopy held up by a man at each corner and preceded by a boy swinging incense censors. Then followed some official of the church chanting in a deep voice, responded to by the sweeter voices of the matrons. [2/6/18]

Another exposure to the Roman Catholic religion occurred shortly afterwards:

Well, here we are in our fifth (dare I say last?) year of war. On Sunday 4th August, the anniversary of that fateful day in 1914 when the war started, we all attended church service in the village 'kirk'. The service was in French and the preacher was, of course, a catholic priest. We have no scruples about attending on religious grounds as the service was held solely in memory of those who had fallen in the war. To a protestant the ceremony was not without interest and the solo songs of one choir girl were worth hearing. [8/8/18]

Life was perhaps a little less rosy for the civilians on the German side of the front. Willie graphically described the depressing aspect of natives in a nearby village which the Allies had taken as the war reached its climax. It is well understood that shortages of food and war materials helped to tip the balance at the end of the war, as the Allied blockade bit deeply, bringing about the final collapse of Germany. The farming communities on the German side must have been stripped of most of their produce and were treated as a subservient enemy in contrast to the Allied side where they were treated as equals, being citizens of partners in the joint struggle against the 'Bosche':

The liberated civilians, what of them? There is a difference between them and their fellow countrymen who have not suffered German rule. They are quieter. They don't seem to realise yet that they are free. One passes groups of them talking in undertones. It is passing off however and one hears more cheery 'bon jours' and 'comment allez vous' every day. [5/11/18]

The exigencies of war had resulted in almost any horse being requisitioned from the local population. It has been claimed that almost as many horses as men perished in the conflict, so although things were quickly getting back to normal once the war was over, the replacement of the equine losses had yet to come into effect:

This town is almost empty of soldiers and, with the gradual influx of its pre-war residents, begins to assume a more normal aspect. Even now one sees peculiar sights, particularly in the transport line. Yoked oxen are to be seen pulling cabs. Today I saw an ox and a horse in double harness pulling a heavy load. Dogs are pressed into service for light loads and not a little haulage depends on man power. For personal transportation the endless stream of army motor vehicles is of wonderful assistance and it has now become uncommon not to see those vehicles without their quota of madams, monsieurs and mademoiselles on board. Out today to Tournai in our own Ford car we picked up a charming female who spoke delightful broken English and informed us that she had returned to France after over four years as a refugee in our own lucky country. [11/5/19]

The last description of the return to normal of French life came in a letter of April 1919. In it Willie describes the scene in a local estaminet:

On opening the door we find ourselves in a room measuring about twenty feet square and having a red tiled floor liberally sprinkled with sand. The door we have entered is in the middle of the front wall between two windows. Before the window on the right one member of the family is cutting hair at threepence a head (an apt term in this connection). The bar is against the centre of the wall left of the front door. It is nothing but a counter three feet from the wall and about six feet long, with a small basin at the side for washing up. Behind this counter is a large mirror with shelves in front for the glasses and surmounted with a stuffed hawk bearing in its beak a wire supporting a glass ball highly coloured and designed to trap flies. Its appearance suggests that it has done well. [28/4/19]

As we have seen, by the end of the war Willie was totally at ease with the language, though as late as May 1918 he had written of linguistic frustrations of an unexpected kind:

Re French studies, the benefit of being in north eastern France and hearing the spoken word are doubtful. The villagers speak a chronic patois which might be an entirely different language from all the sense one can make of it. Every 'S' sound becomes 'sh'; 'comme ça' is 'comme shoo';'de l'eau' sounds like 'de lier'. It is simply atrocious. Even French refugees from other districts seem to have great difficulty in understanding the language. [19/5/18]

Willie spoke his own language with Received Pronunciation and probably did not realise that British people visiting an unfamiliar region of their own country would have just as much difficulty with accents. This would be very true of his home town in east Lancashire. He would understand the local dialect spoken by people untrained in RP, but might have struggled to understand some of the locals in say Somerset or Scotland!

Fluency in French was clearly of great help in his post-Armistice job as orderly room sergeant at headquarters, on his leisure days exploring the liberated battle zone and, later on, holidays in France and Belgium after the war.

17

An Army Without Women

There were no women with the Army in France except for a very few nurses in the base hospitals. The serving soldiers lived in an exclusively masculine society and even the concert parties sent to entertain the troops in the battle zone were all male with some members impersonating females where the sketches required it.

Last night four gentlemen members of the Ashwell concert party came to this village and entertained us admirably. It is stated that this is the only time that a party of English civilians has been allowed so near the trenches. No ladies were allowed to come up however and I think it proved a slight disappointment. One fellow who sat not far from me said that he was dying to see an English tart. [18/2/16]

In the twenty-first century, this situation might give rise in the media to speculation about homosexuality, transvestism and other titillating material. From an early twentieth century perspective however, there was nothing unusual about an all male environment. Homosexuality was a crime and was very severely punished in the armed services. That it was recognised is amply shown by the fact that Oscar Wilde's famous work *A Picture of Dorian Gray* was read by Willie and presumably his comrades, but this form of sexual orientation was seen simply as a curious deviation. Liaisons with local women were not approved and in any case Victorian values were inbred in most young men, though a minority would be subject to more basic instincts.

There certainly were brothels in the bigger towns, but this was probably no more than could be found in larger conurbations anywhere in the world and certainly in British cities.

In truth, women, to the majority of the men under twenty-one years old, being technically still children, meant mother and home as much as girlfriends of their own age. William Whittaker was no exception to the Victorian norm, and indeed was rather prudish in his thoughts about women; any deviation from the strict moral tone of the times simply could not occur to him. Indeed, he was to retain these values all his life as a husband, father and grandfather. The letters contained various references to women, however, and a hint of the temptation they might offer to some soldiers:

As for nice girls, they must not be seen with Tommies, particularly at night. This speaks badly for English soldiers but I think the chief reason is that it is very necessary for the soldier's health and condition. [19/9/15]

In general, most of the girls the soldiers did meet were just normal happy maidens, but not inhibited by their society to express their happiness in an innocent and spontaneous way:

We were about the first English soldiers who had been in that district and our welcome and treatment were therefore of the best. They trusted us in their orchards and we did not take more apples than they wished. When we said goodbye to the healthy buxom lasses we had met in the cafes they kissed us good-humouredly. They were not forward, they kissed us in all pure good feeling and with that spirit of camaraderie which we English seem too cold to give. [28/10/16]

The reality of life without females was well illustrated by a cinema show:

Last night we went to a cinematograph entertainment promoted by the divisional chaplain. Try to imagine an old schoolroom filled with a few plank seats and with a rather dirty screen at one end and you will have an idea or our 'de luxe' picture palace, but it was marvellous. It brought one out of oneself and transported one to civilisation. Whenever a nice girl walked into the picture there was a smacking of lips and a babble of talk which no other incident occasioned. In one scene, where a man was caressing a young babe there was an oppressive silence. The touch of domesticity silenced us all and I suppose it set us thinking of that wonderful place – home. Tears were rolling down the face of a young fellow who sat close to me. You can little imagine how much that little cinematograph show meant to us. In England, an idle amusement by which to pass an hour. Here, a wonderful change from a soldier's life where he never has the comforts or pleasures that a woman can provide. Here, where one's sole companions are men and where one has to work, cook, clean, stitch and provide his own entertainment it was bliss. [1/1/16]

Although the censorship rules prevented him from describing most incidents of death, one of Willie's most vivid recollections about the horror of war was of the many men he saw actually dying from their wounds. With their last breath, he told his own family, they always cried out for their mothers, not for any other relative or friend.

He was very observant and was able to give his parents a shrewd thumbnail sketch of the everyday life and behaviour of French womanhood, on the one hand coping with the shortages brought about by the war, on the other being proud at making themselves smart and attractive:

At a house I visited a few weeks ago the Madame was actually making for herself a new dress from an old army blanket. I have seen the finished article and most people would call me a liar if I asserted that the dress was nothing but a blanket. I also saw the same woman fashion a pretty little frock for her tiny daughter from an army greyback as we call a shirt.

These Frenchwomen seem to have the knack of dressing attractively. I was in a large town near here this morning, Sunday, and was particularly struck by the neat dresses of the ladies. A close inspection would perhaps reveal the cheapness of the material used but this does not alter the fact that the costumes are invariably well made and look good. One seldom sees a dress that is not relieved by some little dash of colour. Even the black mourning dresses, of which there are unfortunately so many, are almost always improved by a little white here and there. I suppose you are very amused by this commentary on ladies' dresses coming from your humble son but really I have been very struck by the well dressed appearance of even the poorest classes.

I should also like to mention the fact that cosmetics, powder and rouge are used by most French females of moderate age. In England one always associates paint and powder with actresses and women of bad repute. It is of course part of these women's business to be attractive. I believe the paint and powder helps to achieve this and proves that these artificial aids are sensible additions. In England a respectable woman is looked down on for employing these means, where Mrs Grundy, that false hypocritical old girl reigns supreme. Yes, France can teach England very much. [28/5/17]

It is clearly inferred from Willie's replies to questions and comments which had been raised in letters from home that there was a misunderstanding in England about the morality of French girls, whose use of cosmetics meant that they were considered nothing more than harpies, determined to seduce and ruin young soldiers:

I used to think, like most Englishmen, that in France most women are immoral. It is decidedly not so. Their immoral women are few and are collected in one district. They are separated and consequently the pure girls are in very small danger of pollution. It would perhaps be better if it were so in

England where Mrs Warren may live next door to an innocent girl and where, as a result, that girl might later become another Mrs Warren. [30/10/16]

The reference was to George Bernard Shaw's famous play *Mrs Warren's Profession* which was, needless to say, prostitution. Shaw, together with Oscar Wilde, was one of the particular authors whose work had been sent to Willie by his parents at his specific request:

There appears to have been much discussion in the papers recently re the French 'Lampe rouge' system. The English people seem to have an entirely erroneous idea of their effect on Tommy. Their existence is an established fact but, impossible as it may appear to those who have followed the newspaper controversy, I and nearly everyone else in the section has not even seen one of these houses. Rather than being a temptation they are surely the reverse for all physically clean persons, not to mention mentally clean persons. That some Tommies have used them I know and that those Tommies will continue to satisfy their desires even if those houses are closed. Being only twenty one years old I write who perhaps should not but I feel it is much better to confine almost inevitable lewdness to regulated houses under medical supervision and situated in as suitable areas as possible, than to allow it to spread in any direction to the disadvantage and detriment of all good clean living people. A decent girl in France knows which areas to avoid to escape molestation. Can an English girl in a garrison town feel similarly secure?

The socialist writer Ernest Marklew in his modernised Ten
Commandments *says 'Thou shalt not indiscreetly commit
adultery, thou sinnest only when found out.' What rot!
yet Mrs Grundy believes, or tries to believe, that what she
doesn't see or doesn't know about doesn't happen. There
has been unchastity since the world began and there will no
doubt be unchastity until the world ends. The French realise
this and have prepared for it. I have no doubt that some
educated English people would wish a similar freedom from
annoyance that the French system gives to its womanhood.*
[1/4/18]

Some of the section, on returning from leave, had been quizzed
on the subject of the allegedly loose morals of Frenchwomen
and had been embarrassed to answer. It is interesting that
even in the twenty-first century there is still a lot of prurient
hypocrisy about the subject of what Willie describes as
'Maisons Tolérées' but then Shaw is not as widely read as the
popular newspapers!

During his frustrating wait for demobilisation after the
Armistice, he did at least enjoy freedom of movement and
the extra pay which he received as a sergeant, and he could
even tell his parents where he was without risking the wrath
of the censor. Shows by the visiting concert parties were less
frequent but they did at last include real women. The troops
also were able to go freely to civilian shows in the French
towns. He summed up the relief at seeing women in a civilian
environment and hearing female voices as part of the growing
normalisation that quickly returned to France:

We had a nice run on the motor bike to Mons, a splendid old town, undamaged by the Bosche, and evidently enjoying a wonderful period of prosperity. The town was 'en fête' to greet the Belgian soldiers who made a triumphant march through the town. The pressed flowers enclosed were thrown on me by a businesslike young lady who sprang from nowhere and said I must buy a flower for the benefit of 'nos héros' – 'combien' I asked. 'Que vous voulez' came the reply and d—n me if I wasn't the poorer by a franc because I had looked in her eyes. Bless my soul they would have drawn francs from a Scotsman.

Just after the above little incident we ran across a Salvation Army hostel from whose doorway the heavenly smell of eggs and chips issued forth. So we went in and ate the eggs and chips to the noise of the chatter of the English girls who were serving and believe me it is a good many months since I realised how sweet the English language is when fallen from the lips of the ladies.

Then we walked around the town past fine restaurants and splendid shops until the pubs opened, when, with so much of the Mons dust in our throats, dust which should be worth a guinea an ounce to the souvenir hunters, we dispelled it with a bottle of real English beer – BASS. I've spelt it in capitals because that is how it felt. I count it as among the most enjoyable days I have spent on active service. [7/4/19]

Willie was also able to observe and appreciate the domestic hardships caused by the disruption of the war on the day-to-day lives of Frenchwomen and their fortitude in bearing them:

It has been borne on me, during retrospective periods, how much more some of the French women are enduring than our most sacrificing English women. Some of the French women I say for I speak only of those women who inhabit that triangular piece of northern France which has Boulogne for its apex and the battle front for its base. This area is overrun with English but yet they are foreigners even though so numerous. To illustrate my point I must give you now an example of what happens to a French householder in this area. Suppose Burnley was in the war zone (how I thank providence that it is not) our house would be on the billeting list. You would be visited by some official who would say how many soldiers you were to accommodate. You would perhaps have to give two bedrooms and the sitting room for them and shelter maybe twenty men. In the army there are many thoughtless and therefore unthankful men and among your twenty there would be some who ungratefully failed to recognise what inconvenience you were being put to. Your own home comforts would inevitably disappear and your recompense would be inadequate. Furthermore your proximity to the line would put your life and property in danger. The women of the triangular portion of France mentioned have these conditions thrust upon them and have also given their husbands and sons to the cause, just as you.

I think I have succeeded in proving that a great many French women are enduring more than Englishwomen but I have not heard, except in isolated cases, any grumbling from them. So I give my four toasts for the new year in this order:

To peace with victory
To you my dear parents
To all my soldier comrades and friends at home
AND
To the women of France [4/1/18]

18

Home Comforts

Whatever shortcomings in the military tactics that the Allied commanders in the First World War have been accused of, they certainly did many useful things to improve morale. The beneficial effects of good health and hygiene, the plentiful supply of wholesome food, the regular high-quality entertainment provided, and even the understandable use of mild propaganda all helped to maintain good spirits, even in the face of appalling danger and often poor living conditions.

A further aspect of the thought behind these measures to keep Tommy happy was in the incredible efficiency of the postal service. Letters and parcels from families and friends in Britain normally reached the men serving at the front within two days – and there was no air mail! The parcels almost invariably contained the universally smoked and craved for cigarettes, sweets and other foodstuffs. It was even possible to send fresh food items without them going off and in this very real way the troops were kept in meaningful contact with home.

Another aspect of home comfort was the determination of millions of women, who were not allowed to volunteer for military service, to do their bit. This took many forms but the dominating solution was the formation of knitting parties or sewing bees to provide handmade articles of clothing for the boys on active service. It is not surprising that a woolly scarf was known as a 'comforter'.

Tom and Bella Whittaker sent their son a parcel at least once a week and letters even more frequently. Nearly all Willie's replies begin with thanks for the letters, parcel or sometimes parcels and newspapers received. The parcels always contained cigarettes and food, and a regular feature was the *Burnley Express* newspaper and cuttings from other papers and journals about the war so that he was always kept up to date with local news and the sentiment among the civilian population in England.

There were many other home comforts in the parcels, usually items specifically requested but sometimes unsolicited. The host of useful items, all mentioned in the letters, included:

Notepads, pencils and envelopes
Books, novels, treatises and text books
Toiletries such as soap and toothpaste
Additional smoking materials such as a pipe and cigars
Air pillows
Musical items, a violin, strings, sheet music
A purse
Dishcloths
Cocoa
Boot brushes
Khaki thread
A luminous wrist watch

Willie was an avid reader and constantly requested improving literature to widen his general knowledge and education and also to broaden his mind and develop his philosophy on war, politics and life:

I should be pleased to receive a copy of Cobbet's Grammar *if this is not too expensive. It will also be much to my advantage if I get a firm grip of the subject. [1/9/16]*

I was pleased to receive your parcel today and look forward to a few pleasant hours, when I have time, along with the music. I should be very much obliged if you would send me out Today *regularly as it seems to be a very good publication. Also please enclose in the next parcel* Man and Superman *and* The Doctor's Dilemma, *both sixpenny paperbacks by George Bernard Shaw which you will find in the book cupboard. [13/5/16]*

This literature was freely passed among the comrades and must have provoked lively discussion of such topics as the emerging realisation of the changing role of women so cleverly portrayed in Shaw's masterpiece *Man and Superman* and the political changes subtly outlined in his *An Unusual Socialist*:

Cannon, a profound Conservative, and pronounced by his lifetime friend Mills to be a snob, read An Unusual Socialist *and enjoyed it and has a great desire to read more Shaw. [13/5/16]*

Willie repeatedly asked for the non-food items to be paid for out of the tiny remittance he sent home weekly out of his meagre pay. He also asked his parents to take money out of his savings to buy a present whenever either of them had a birthday. When he was demobbed, however, he found that every penny he had sent had been kept in a savings account, untouched, and which, with some interest, provided him with a useful nest egg to ease himself back into civilian life.

One interesting thing about the parcels is the number of occasions when they included items gifted by friends, neighbours and relatives. Typical presents were an extra packet of cigarettes, a bag of sweets or sometimes a cake. Willie never failed to send his thanks for these items, either via his parents or by a letter sent directly to the donor. Relatives such as Cousin Rachel and names of kind people such as a Mrs Duerden or a Mrs Wilkinson occur from time to time. On one occasion there must have been several donors as he sent thanks to 'All who had contributed to the parcel'.

Then there were the homemade clothes, sometimes sent from friends and sometimes by the knitters and sewers:

I was surprised today to receive a letter and parcel from 'Lollie' Atkinson, containing two pairs of socks and a fine thick muffler. I think it is very kind to send presents like that. [25/10/15]

The letter from Mr Atkinson, Willie's old Sunday school teacher, was enclosed for Tom and Bella to read and was from an address in St Annes-on-Sea. He sent similar parcels to all the North Street lads who were serving. Mr Atkinson's letters always included a prayer for them.

Other organisations sent comforts:

The other day we were fortunate recipients of parcels from the London Daily Chronicle. *We have also received a large box of comforts from some kirk in Scotland containing scarves, body belts, mittens, sleeping helmets, socks, shirts etc.* [20/11/15]

Please post the enclosed letters. They are thanks for socks received as winter comforts. Each man in the section got three pairs of socks, one muffler and a pair of mittens, all in good thick wool. Here is the card which was attached to the socks. [12/11/17]

The card was headed with the printed civic crest of the borough of Southport, the message was handwritten and read:

Southport War Comforts Committee
This article was made by –
Miss A. Belcher
69A the Promenade
Southport
August 1917

With best wishes and may you come back to dear old Blighty safely to the old folks at home.

Willie's reply thanked Miss Belcher and enclosed a photograph, and this sparked off a brief exchange of letters between them and for a time she was added to his extensive list of correspondents:

Miss Belcher has replied to my letter including the photograph and promises to send me one of her photos as soon as she has one taken. She has also invited me to spend a day at Southport when next on leave. She has prepared me for her photograph by saying that when I see her physiognomy I will jump right over the top. [16/2/18]

This letter is my fourteenth during the past few days so you will understand I have been well occupied. I have written to uncle John, Worsthorne church, Willie Greenwood and Mrs Hodgson and to Miss Belcher, diplomatically asking her age. [1/2/17]

This elicited a reply with a rather wistful tone. It seems it must have been sent unsealed via his parents so that they read it, hence the following comment from Willie:

Let me assure you that I have not offended the susceptibilities of Miss Belcher for only yesterday I received a cheery letter and a few of her special cigarettes, Saxony silk tipped Egyptians etc. May I quote a little? 'No mon cher you are not writing to a damsel of eighteen, nor my goodness to an old maid of eighty. It may someday be an inappropriate blessing. One never knows, does one? All the same it is very sweet to have a friend even on paper if young or old. As you may imagine I have passed the fine youth of girlhood and one day we may meet on the promenade.' [4/1/18]

Miss Belcher kindly sent me a magazine and a packet of Abdullah No. 16 cigarettes with good wishes for Eastertide. I am rather looking forward to meeting this extraordinary Miss who displays such kindness to one comparatively unknown acquaintance. I hardly think she is a servant at 69A, in fact, a few moments consideration makes one almost sure:

1. A person of education would not, during the present time of high wages and employment for women be concerned with the mere existence which is the lot of the lowly paid servant.

2. A servant would hardly be in a position to buy magazines at ninepence and Abdullah No.16 at goodness knows what price.

No, she is not a servant but of course I do not intend to ask her to enlighten me for she may assume that I desire to possess greater intimacy than is the fact, though really one cannot help but be interested. [1/4/18]

Miss Belcher sent a seaside postcard bearing a fine picture of No. 69A The Promenade. It was a handsome property, stone built and evidently the home of wealthy people. There was one further mention of Miss Belcher in the letters to the effect that no photograph had been received and perhaps Willie was scared off by the hint that he might seek her out after the war. In any case she seems to have been quickly forgotten. Her kindness was, however, typical of the spirit of so many women who helped to give the boys reminders of home.

So all these gifts went some small way to bridge the gap between home and foreign field, but after his parents what did Willie miss most? His dog!

Dogs were a principle hobby of Tom Whittaker. He kept a pedigree show dog and entered him in competitions all over Lancashire. Terry, an Irish terrier, won countless prizes, and one of Tom's most treasured possessions was a collection of prize tickets as thick as a pack of cards. Some were 'Best in Show', some 'Champion' and some 'First' and 'Reserve'. During the First World War, the family dog was Jenny, whose exact breed is unfortunately never mentioned although we know that she was a small terrier. Willie missed Jenny badly and referred to her in the most affectionate terms, especially in the early days, when homesickness must have been most intense:

Good luck to dear little doggie – bless it. [10/8/15]
Kisses for little Jenny. [2/9/15]
I should like a photo of little Jenny. [2/11/15]
I have received the snapshot of 'her nibs'. Faulty though it is it brings back, each time I look at it, a thousand memories of home. [2/11/15]

Much later Jenny became pregnant:

I am glad to hear that Jenny is alright. I hope she successfully surmounts the dangers of maternity and that after this you will see that she has exercise enough to prevent her development into a pot-bellied hearth rug dog. I have often thought she must be suffering without the exercise of the runs I used to give her nearly every summer day. [3/5/17]

The outcome of the pregnancy must have been fully documented in the letters from home but none survive and Willie made no comment about the litter. He himself never had a dog after he left home following his demobilisation, but he talked to his family about the devotion of Jenny, without ever mentioning her breed! When he had his last leave, just before demob, the family pet had not seen him for two whole years. He recalled that as he walked through the door Jenny raced ahead of his parents and threw herself at him in a frenzy of joyful recognition.

The section did adopt stray dogs in France, which must have gone some way to fill the gap left by the separation from Jenny:

Enclosed is a snap taken by the officer at St Amand some months ago. I may be seen lighting a fag. Phillips and the section dog Jim, who has been with us for three and a half years, is with me. [7/7/19]

Jim was mentioned in more than one letter and must have been with them since early in 1916, based at the St Amand headquarters. They adopted another stray in Flanders, appropriately called 'Wipers', the soldier's pronunciation of Ypres:

We have a little refugee dog named Wipers which always makes me think of Jenny, it being a small terrier. If only it was my little Jenny. [27/10/17]

Naturally, though, Willie most of all missed his parents, regularly commenting on their minor ailments and their problems in coping with the deprivations brought about in England by the war. He especially missed his father. The following extract is rather cryptic but clearly demonstrates that he was missing the wise counsel of Tom Whittaker:

I have read and digested father's letter. I recognise the limitations in correspondence and I do wish I could have a long talk with you. [8/4/18]

Again the one-sided nature of the correspondence means that the issues he wished to discuss are not stated. It is easy to see however that any young man would often wish to be able to confide to someone closer than his immediate comrades.

Nothing, absolutely nothing, could properly replace the comforts of home sweet home.

19

Leave

Leave, or rather the prospect of it, was a preoccupation for every man on active service in France. It dominated conversation and was by far the most frequently mentioned issue in correspondence.

It is revealing that the granting of leave, quite clearly the best possible way of raising morale, was for other ranks a rare occurrence, though officers seemed to fare much better. Much care and attention was paid to the other morale-raising factors, health and hygiene, good food, quality entertainment and an efficient postal service, but why was not leave awarded more frequently?

A reading of some of the political and military histories of the war perhaps provides an answer. Earl Haig and the British High Command were convinced that a major part of the equation which would bring about victory was a numbers game – more guns, more shells, and most importantly more men. Demands were constantly made for reinforcements and the more damning of the histories suggest that men were regarded as cannon fodder as they were ordered over the top to face the hail of German rifle and machine-gun fire which awaited them at every battle or attempted advance. They seemed to think that it was always going to be better next time and to shrug off the colossal number of casualties in the knowledge that the dead and wounded could be replaced by new conscripts.

The leave arrangements for the infantry were evidently on a block system with whole units being relieved at the same time and shipped on leave trains to Boulogne en route to Folkestone. For a specialised unit like 41st Sanitary Section, leave was always a question of lists. The theory was that every so often a list would open and one, two or sometimes three lucky men would, in turn, get a leave pass to Blighty. The length of the pass was usually one week, which would mean six days at home. This was on the face of it a sensible arrangement for a group engaged in constant work to ensure that hygiene was kept up, water supplies rendered safe and always available, waste disposed of and other sanitary arrangements supervised. There would always be sufficient men on duty to ensure continuity.

The problem was that the rota rarely completed a full cycle. Officers got home a couple of times a year. Senior NCOs were given preference, married men were moved up the list, compassionate cases occurred and worst of all, the slightest activity on the front, let alone a major battle or push, led to all leave being cancelled. In one letter Willie, who got leave only three times in four years, one of those after the Armistice, wryly commented that his officer had just got back from his third leave. A typical description of how it did – or more frequently did not – operate, occurred in one of the early letters:

Re leave, I have no idea at all of when I shall be able to get away. Every day brings to us some new rumour. For instance, one day we were told that two are going each week until finished. Another day we hear that leave has been stopped for six weeks and today I was told that the Assistant Director of medical services was only allowed to send three each week from his companies which include the ambulances, the travelling workshop section and ourselves, altogether about a thousand men. Leave is an everyday topic of conversation and from the very first day a soldier sets foot in France he seems to look forward to that wonderful leave. [18/12/15]

Several times the letters included phrases like 'with any luck I will be with you in a few weeks after x, y and z have had their leave as I am now fourth on the list to go', only for all leave to be stopped. No reason was ever given for leave being stopped, no doubt for security reasons. Other letters displayed a more optimistic note:

Sergeant Gooding and Staff Sergeant Gawthorpe are now on leave and we are all anxiously awaiting the next leave grant which may give us an idea as to the date of our own lucky week. Rumours are strong that we shall get through the leave very quickly, in which case I hope to be home towards the end of next month but do not expect me until you get a telegram from Euston. I also ask you to mention leave as little as possible in your letters to me. You are no more anxious than I that I should get leave soon but a continued reminder and questions about leave becomes monotonous. You can trust

me to let you know immediately I have any definite news.
[7/1/16]

Obviously genuine strategic reasons had to override the personal convenience of any soldier but when one reflects that there were many false alarms and that the offensives which did occur were almost always virtual stalemates in which tens of thousands lost their lives, the judgement of those in political authority and the general staff has been questioned by many commentators. Morale of the troops remained high in spite of their frustrations as the men did not let their disappointment at the postponement of leave deflect them from their belief in what they were doing and their dogged determination to defeat 'Jerry'. Willie never complained and took all the vicissitudes calmly and philosophically and got on with the job.

When he saw infantrymen going on leave and coming back from it, the young sanitary engineer wrote a powerful and deeply thoughtful piece about just how much leave meant to the troops. The section had just arrived by train at St Omer railway station to take up duties in a new area:

On arrival at the station, which had a magnificent appearance, we saw the leave train departing. It was a big train and very crowded. Every face was covered in a smile. They had not the ordinary smile which one sees after some amusing incident. No, in every case it was a smile of anticipation, anticipation of the pleasures which Blighty held for them. It did one good to see these lucky blighters, as a soldier near to me dubbed his more fortunate colleagues. They were nearly all singing

*'Keep the home fires burning' and the last line of the song
'Till the boys come home' rang out of the carriages as the
train departed.*

*What thoughts crowded into my brain. I have never in
all my life realised how much home and parental sympathy,
encouragement and help meant. These soldiers, some of whom
had just come out of the terrible fighting line, would be in
England in less than twenty four hours. They would be enjoying
comforts which now mean so much to them after the strenuous
and utterly uncomfortable times they have had out here.*

*At our next station we met the train which had brought
back men who had returned from leave via Boulogne. Their
songs were of the 'Are we downhearted' type. Their final 'No'
at the end of the line seemed to ring false and I remember one
young fellow, who was singing as loudly as ever, saying it felt
b—y awful coming back to this rotten place. The life here
must feel many times harder for those who have just returned
from leave, even harder than when they first came out for then
they advanced to the danger zone very slowly, some being in
France over a month before they heard the sound of guns,
whilst now, on returning from leave, they are carried straight
from Boulogne to the trenches. [8/1/17]*

Most of the hopes of imminent leave were dashed but Willie's
first leave pass came in the spring of 1916. In anticipation he
thought through his plans for his homecoming:

*You can trust me to get to Burnley as soon as possible. You
also asked me how I intend to pass my time, who I intend to*

see and where I intend to go. Well, the very fact of passing my time in England in almost any manner will be better than the best of times out here. I do not intend to go anywhere especially, though I shall make every effort to see all my friends and acquaintances. [14/2/16]

The leave was actually postponed because of an outbreak of measles in the Burnley area and no soldier was allowed to go there in case he brought the disease back with him. Willie even thought of giving a fictitious address for his travel pass but decided against it. However the date was not long delayed and the weather would probably have been kinder in April than in February:

I now know, officially, that my leave will start on Thursday April 6th. I may succeed in catching the 12.00 noon boat and should reach London at 4.00 p.m. This being so I will probably reach Burnley about midnight. If the weather is bad it may be Friday or even Saturday and secondly, mines sometimes break loose in the Channel and then the boats are stopped. One also never knows when leave might be stopped for many reasons. I mention all these things to remind you not to expect me till I telegram from Euston. [1/4/16]

The telegram was duly sent from Euston station and was carefully preserved among the letters. There is no record of what he actually did on leave but the journey back to France and its aftermath were well covered in his first letter on return:

I address my letter once again from flowery France. I have heard France spoken of in different terms but today everything seems freshly pretty. A good hot sun is pouring down on our tents and I feel very drowsy. Even the guns seem to be asleep and the hum of the aeroplanes comes down to us very dully. The bell of the church is summoning people to their devotions and everything makes it difficult to believe that war is so near. I arrived in camp at 2.00 a.m. along with Haldane whom I met in Folkestone. Woolfe, having caught an earlier train, was able to reach camp yesterday. I reached Folkestone at 12.30 and was taken into rest camp until 8.30 in the evening. The rest camp at Folkestone is not at all a bad place. The government has walled in a three or four hundred yard stretch of the promenade, including the boarding houses and hotels of the Marine Parade as it is named. These houses are empty of furniture and are used for the troops. I had a lovely bed sitting room commanding a splendid view of the sea and, the weather being good, I enjoyed my stay fine. We were allowed out in the afternoon and had the opportunity to wander all around the town. I spent some time laid on the pebbly beach and, dozing with the sound of the sea in my ears, found it very easy mentally to reconstruct the details of many happy holidays in less troubled times. The wind began to freshen and at 8.30, when we set sail, the sea was choppy and almost everyone was seasick. We were packed like sardines and you can imagine how uncomfortable it was.

Fortunately neither Haldane nor I fell prey to the pangs of this miserable illness. Reaching Boulogne at about 10.30 we were marched off up a tremendous hill to another rest camp and bundled into tents, twelve in each. Each man was given a blanket and told to parade at 6.30 a.m. the following morning. We paraded as ordered but were then dismissed with further instructions to parade at 5.30 p.m. We succeeded in getting into town and had a good look around. My roast chicken passed away at this camp and was very welcome. At 5.25 we were marched down to the railway station, packed into the miserable French carriages and left Boulogne at 8.30 p.m. We arrived at our station at about 1.30 a.m., marched to our headquarters and thus completed our leave experience. [16/4/16]

A new list was prepared about a year later. It was exactly on his twentieth birthday that Willie wrote pessimistically, as the spring campaigning season, when most military activity took place, was expected to start soon:

The leave barometer has dropped a little this last fortnight, there having been only one pass per week instead of two as before. Little occurrences of this sort may prevent some of us from having leave at all for I am certain that leave will be discontinued on the arrival of spring. [22/1/17]

Kilburn's leave has been delayed five days and six others have to go before I do, always taking for granted that we observe the same order as last year. [5/2/17]

No one has gone from the section since Kilburn but I understand leave is to start again in a day or two. I do not think I shall be lucky enough to enjoy this privilege. He who expecteth nothing shall not be disappointed. [25/2/17]

Leave has opened again but only at a very slow rate. Our lorry driver has gone this morning after twenty one months in France without leave. To be candid I do not expect leave. I think I shall have to wait until 'après la guerre' before I see you again. [28/5/17]

Latest leave bulletin:
Lanham is expected back today.
Johnson left here last Tuesday.
Babb will probably go on leave on the 3rd.
Phillips is due the week after.
Bradley has gone into hospital with some skin disease and may miss his turn.

This may put me a week forward and cause my leave to commence about the 19th. Law has accompanied Bradley into hospital, both suffering from the same complaint. I paraded sick with them, also suffering from a similar outbreak of sores on the face. Fortunately my disfigurement is rapidly disappearing and I am carrying on my work as usual. So we are two men short and even busier than ever. I deeply fear that leave will be stopped until some reinforcements arrive. Your suggestion of a day or two at the seaside if I come home echoes my desires, but more anon. [1/1/17]

Leave has stopped! Phillips left nine days ago and my pass had come in when leave was stopped. Bradley is back from hospital and will be the first to go when leave recommences. [19/7/17]

The pessimism thus seemed well founded but all finished well. The latest delay cannot have lasted long for the list was duly completed and he got leave after all. Unfortunately this must have happened very quickly as there was no further mention of it until he was back in France after a spell in Blighty:

I was late in London after three changes, arriving at 7.15 a.m. Leaving at 7.30 I reached Folkestone and despatched a postcard to you. We had a few hours there which we spent easily on the beach, dozing. We left at 2.30 and reached France at 4.30 after a wobbly sort of crossing. We stayed the night at Boulogne and entrained the following morning, reaching our station at about 4.30 yesterday. I have been working this morning but am suffering from the most acute attack of homesickness I have ever had. It will no doubt disappear gradually as the more vivid pictures of my days in England fade. [19/8/17]

The postcard from Folkestone survives and bears a coloured photograph of the Marine Parade in happier times before it was requisitioned.

Willie was now at a busy mining town, Bruay, and actually spelt out its full name. It is not clear whether the censorship rules now allowed this practice though the letters continued to be headed simply 'Somewhere in France'. One of the travelling concert parties visited the town. Willie attended and recounted a very wry joke told by a ventriloquist and his doll:

Doll: I say guvnor, can you tell me what is the difference between trees and soldiers?

Ventriloquist: No, what's the difference?
Doll: Well, trees have leaves. [1/9/17]

A list was again opened a year later, with NCOs getting preference as usual:

Leave has started. Sergeant Leslie goes tomorrow. Corporal Lott is expected to go next week and bar accidents leave is expected to continue at the rate of one man per week. Without taking into account the almost inevitable stoppages I should be home early in May. [29/1/18]

Corporal Lott has returned from leave. Jack Clark goes tomorrow and it is hoped that leave will continue at the same rate of one per week. I am about the tenth on the list after Clark but leave has a nasty habit of stopping at times for a full month or longer. [29/2/18]

Moore has gone on leave today and it is hoped that this month we shall send one each week. The order of going is now Black, Lanham, Williamson, Johnson, Babb, Phillips, Bradley and Whittaker. But let me say that nothing is certain in wartime. [5/3/18]

This list was never completed. The final desperate push by the Germans and the Allied response, now reinforced by the Americans and troops of other Allied armies, caused all leave to be cancelled. Willie did not get home again until six months after the war had ended and his third and last leave featured anxious casting about for job opportunities and the purchase of a civilian suit with interviews in mind. The practice of giving demobbed servicemen a suit free of charge, well established after the Second World War, had not yet begun.

Unfortunately there is no record, as usual, of exactly what he did when he was at home on leave as it was not news to his parents. There is again only the record of his journey back to France:

I reached London at about 4 o'clock on the 27th May and stayed at the central YMCA in Tottenham Court Road, wandered down Charing Cross Road and along Shaftsbury Avenue to Leicester Square, trying to decide which theatre to visit in the evening. I finally booked a seat at the London Pavilion for the revue As You Were *starring Alice Delisia and John Humphries. It was simply fine, the wonderful dresses and tuneful music being particularly splendid.*

I had a good night's rest at the YM and left Victoria at 8.30 with Haldane, who I luckily met on the station. We had an hour or two on the leas at Folkestone, listening to the orchestra and after a beautiful crossing reached Calais at 5.00 p.m., where we stayed the night, then via Pernes and St Pol, where we stayed another night before getting back to base for breakfast. [30/5/19]

Willie was to get a good lifetime job without difficulty. His promotion to sergeant and the valuable office work he did after the Armistice resulted in a glowing testimonial from his officer when the great day of demobilisation arrived and paradoxically the delay in obtaining his discharge worked out well in the end.

20

Demobilisation

Most people thought that the conflict would be a short one when war was declared in August 1914. The volunteers thought it would last no longer than 1916 and dismissed as irrelevant that they were signing on for three years or the duration. As the war dragged on, however, demobilisation became a serious issue. It was not just the wish in the heart of every soldier to get back home to Blighty, which at first seemed like an end in itself, but also the growing preoccupation in the minds of those men who did not have a guaranteed job to go back to with the need to secure employment. This became a gnawing worry for the majority of the men, those who had survived the slaughter and had no job waiting for them in civilian life.

In 1914, the Victorian social order and accepted mode of behaviour were very much still in force even though it was Victoria's grandson King George V who was on the throne. The war saw fundamental changes which would no doubt have evolved slowly under peacetime conditions but which were accelerated dramatically by the conflict.

The departure of so many men into the armed services left huge gaps in the labour force and the shortfall in manpower was exacerbated by the insatiable requirement for munitions. This required the manufacture of naval and military hardware such as ships, aircraft, artillery, rifles and eventually tanks, but even more significantly, ammunition such as shells, bullets and grenades.

The only readily available labour force was women, and although most working-class girls worked in the textile and food processing industries and in domestic service, it was still the norm for women to adopt the household role of wife and mother on marriage.

The munitions factories soaked up female labour to fill shells and bullets with explosives. Women were also needed to add to the agricultural labour force and, for the better educated, to do clerical work. This all provided dramatic momentum for female emancipation, the working out of which was to be a dominant theme in society throughout the twentieth century.

On the political front the war accelerated the growth of the Labour movement which was to challenge the dominance of the Conservative and Liberal parties. A fundamental change in social attitudes, regardless of vested interests, was inevitable with the consequent breaking of the long established mould of British politics.

After the Armistice in 1918 the issue of demobilisation loomed large. There was no quick release for any soldier not in a special category. Married men, skilled men, older men and those with a guaranteed job to go back to all had precedence. They were known as 'slip' men because they were quickly eased back into civilian life. The fundamental issue facing a soldier who ticked none of the special boxes was that there were fewer jobs back in Britain anyway, as the armaments factories were run down or converted into less labour-intensive units. Many women, with the independence brought about by having a regular wage of their own, were not going to give up their jobs lightly and in any case, there was a great shortage of marriage partners because of the decimation of a generation of young men killed in the war. Another factor is that women were paid lower wages than men and employers had a sound reason for keeping women on the payroll.

Like so many working-class girls, Bella Whittaker had worked as a winder in a Burnley cotton mill from the age of twelve until her marriage but then, after raising her son, returned to the mill for a brief period during the war. Indeed in one letter, after his mother had been ill with flu, Willie suggested that although the money was useful, she should give up work.

Although he had believed that he had a guaranteed job, Willie's hopes were dashed and he had no claim to early demobilisation once the war ended. To add to the delaying factors, he was so competent and reliable in his new clerical duties as senior orderly room sergeant that there was a vested interest by his superiors, regular Army officers, to keep him in the Army in France for as long as possible.

His first job, on leaving school at the age of fourteen, was working for his uncle John Whittaker, a debt collector. He then worked for the local newspaper as a runner and became a lifelong supporter of Burnley football club as he got to see part of their home matches free on a Saturday afternoon. His humble task was to run between the ground and the newspaper office three or four times a game with an up-to-date copy, as written by the reporter at the match, so that the various editions of the evening paper would have the latest score and highlights of the game to date. There was no electronic transmission in those days!

Then he got what he thought was a career job, as a junior clerk in the Burnley County Court, where his boss was a Mr Napthen, the chief clerk. Willie was delighted to receive a warm letter from him in November 1915, shortly after his arrival in France. The letter contained day-to-day news of old colleagues and the goings on at the court. He specifically said how much he had missed Willie's help in sorting out the annual accounts. Napthen apologised for not volunteering himself for the Army but he was a married man and his employers would not give him permission to join up.

In the light of subsequent events, the letter contained the prescient comment that there was a great shortage of clerks and a lot of young ladies were being employed, many of whom were to keep their jobs after the war. Willie wrote to Mr Napthen from time to time and as late as 1918, he was still confident of returning to the county court:

I have asked Mr Napthen if he has any old books relating to court work which he thinks might be to my advantage to peruse, bearing in mind the rapidly approaching termination of the war (how's that for optimism!). [26/2/18]

One must not grumble for the County Court will be very busy after the war and the chances will without doubt be plentiful. [4/2/15]

It is my opinion that the courts will be busy après la guerre. It has always seemed to me that a government job, if one is steady and industrious, is almost a sinecure and is usually remunerative. I have told Mr Napthen that I will certainly keep an open mind as to future occupation but that, as and when I again don 'civvies' I shall need to start something and I trust that I may be able to make myself useful at the court at least until I get my wind so to speak. [11/3/18]

Willie toyed with other ways of earning a living. His father suggested that he use his musical skill and Willie replied:

Having in mind that uncle James was at one time an attraction as a singer I cannot but think that whatever talent I may possess in the musical line may possibly come in handy. [10/6/18]

In fact, the violin came in as a very useful earner, as a supplement to his day job, after demobilisation. Willie secured a job in the 'pit' at a Burnley cinema, the Tivoli, playing in a three-piece band of violin, piano and drums as an accompaniment to the silent movies. 'Talkies' had not yet been invented and most cinemas could only afford a pianist but the Tivoli did it in style. With the reels of each new film there came a musical score and the professional musicians would play from it virtually at sight at the first showing! He was able to save up enough money from his fiddle-playing to get married.

There was also talk of applying to the Birkenhead brewery, that establishment being only a few miles from Tarvin in Cheshire where Tom and Bella Whittaker, having recently moved from Burnley, were now mine hosts at a tied public house of the brewery, the George and Dragon. Willie even toyed with the idea of a bit of freelance journalism but he was not keen to chase after another full-time job because he still felt secure in the employment he believed was guaranteed at the county court:

The pleasant fact remains that I have a job to go back to at the County Court. Mr Napthen admitted it when I saw him last. It may offer an easy and lucrative job after the war and I have thought recently that there may be opportunities of transferring say to Manchester County Court. [1/11/18]

Hopes of an early demob were dashed. Only a few days after the Armistice, Willie contracted a mild dose of 'flu' and was sent to the base hospital, which could have been a quick route back to civvy street:

Just two days ago I was the most miserable creature who ever formed fours. Twenty two of us, all cured influenza cases, paraded in front of the doctor to be examined preparatory to what is termed 'marking out'. I, poor, miserable, unlucky I, was the only unfortunate individual who was not marked HSD, meaning Hospital Ship Deck, meaning Blighty. My heart wept great big hugging tears of unalloyed misery. I quickly found some consoling balm. Most of the momentarily lucky were suffering from debility and weak heart action. I was fit! It is a consolation to be told you are fit. The section is applying for my return so I hope it comes off. [25/11/18]

Then came a shattering letter from Mr Napthen saying that after all, there was not going to be a job at the county court when Willie was demobbed. The letters home now contained requests for Tom Whittaker to write asking for an early release and to look around for a job in the Chester area. He had passed an examination for the post office and was at least confident of a good reference from Mr Napthen, who was now regarded as perfidious. He was however assured of good references from the Army:

I consider the County Court have played a dirty trick, having had nothing from Mr Napthen since sending my last letter. [18/12/18]

I have confidentially written my former colleague Arthur Bracknell asking him to turn up any orders issued by the court authorities at the commencement of war stating that re-employment would obtain for those joining up. I am sure there were statements to that effect. If so, I shall state that there is definite employment awaiting me and so make myself eligible for release as a slip man. Meanwhile nothing will be lost by keeping a roving eye out in the vicinity of Chester. [21/12/18]

I have received a reply from Arthur Bracknell in which he proves a ready friend by giving me the assistance of his memory and access to County Court information (confidentially of course) by confirming that re-employment was promised when I enlisted. He expresses surprise at the apparent indifference of

Mr Napthen and suggests that he has deliberately misconstrued the last order issued by the Treasury which said that 'Vacancies are not to be filled without the sanction of the Treasury'. Arthur says that vacancies created by men enlisting had not to be filled by the employment of substitutes, an entirely different meaning. [7/1/19]

Mr Napthen, who had found an excuse not to be called up, was evidently not to be relied on and perhaps Willie was lucky not to have become his subordinate:

Enclosed please find Mr Napthen's letter. He is a liar, no, let me put it another and more polite way. He is under the impression that he told me that I had annulled my chances of reinstatement in 1915. It is a totally wrong impression as Arthur Bracknell in a recent letter to me stated that throughout the war he had held the idea that my job was open pending my return. However, I have diplomatically told Mr Napthen that the mistake is no doubt on my side and requested that he will send me a testimonial to further my efforts in some other direction. [2/2/19]

The priority now switched from the county court to the Civil Service. Willie had been diligently studying the mathematics and English text books which his father had sent him in the expectation that he would be sitting an examination for entry. At least Mr Napthen did send a testimonial and some advice about the Civil Service, which did not prove helpful as Willie had already applied:

I have written to both the Ministry of Labour and the Civil Service Commission with respect to getting a government appointment by competitive selection. Despite these efforts on my part please pursue the enquiries as requested. You may discover how the wind blows in Chester and what chances there are of getting a Civil Service job there. [12/2/19]

Willie went ahead with his application, saying that the scheme was the opportunity of a lifetime. He requested various documents from home including school leaving certificates and dates of attending evening classes in Burnley as well as notification that he had passed the post office exam before joining up:

I have had a reply with reference to the Civil Service selection board and my letter was evidently sufficiently satisfactory as they have sent back forms to fill in on which I am instructed to say in what branch of the Civil Service I would like an appointment and in which district I prefer to work. The commencing salary for a junior post is £150 p.a. and on enquiry I have discovered that a smart fellow may, with effort, reach a salary of £750 p.a. in due course. If my application is satisfactory it may be months after my demobilisation before I am called before the selection board and I shall be compelled to pass an examination. A start of £150 is tempting and a prospect of £750 is dazzling so I intend to return the forms and to state that I would like to enter the Customs and Excise and to work in or near the county of Cheshire. [18/2/19]

The list of subjects included in the examination was quite comprehensive: handwritten English, including essays and précis writing, arithmetic, and general knowledge including scientific, geographic and political affairs. References were also required from his Army commanding officer and a civilian source so Mr Napthen might have come in useful after all! The Civil Service Commission replied with more forms to complete and giving a date of 9 September 1919 for examination at a centre of the candidate's choice.

These bright prospects of employment apparently disappeared and unfortunately the letters do not reveal why as there was no further reference. When he got a long leave in June 1919, shortly before his demobilisation, he evidently saw or contacted the Civil Service and must have been discouraged:

I am not miserable or depressed. I just feel intensely indignant and badly treated. I almost feel wild enough to pass on my information to Horatio Bottomley except that it would be futile and childish. [6/6/19]

The letters after the leave refer to news which his parents must have had verbally when he was at home, for the first letter after his return to France hints at some kind of favouritism in the selection procedure:

I agree with you that nothing is likely to be gained by commencing further correspondence with the Commissioners. The idea of writing to the socialist M.P. for Burnley is better.

I've a good mind to write to Dan. The government, a self called democratic parliament, seems to allow class prejudice to exist in a department under its control. [7/7/19]

The same letter goes on to indicate a real fear of not having a job but at the same time determination to find something. Willie must have contacted the county court yet again during his leave for a possibility of returning to his old job seems to have occurred in spite of all the previous rejections. The letter below contains a cryptic reference so perhaps an unexpected vacancy had occurred, Arthur Bracknell had intervened or Mr Napthen had a change of heart or re-read the instructions more sympathetically:

I am touched by your kind offer to keep me in grub etc. but I am sure you will see that that sort of thing is absolutely out of the question. I see no sense in being dependent on the dole. If nothing better turns up I can return to the County Court and there, even if the pay is not much bigger than the dole I shall become reacquainted with civilian occupation. [7/7/19]

Demobilisation was now imminent. The last letters recount how some of the remaining team from the 41st Sanitary Section went home and quote a directive saying that the last men in the section were all to be demobbed by the end of July. The new suit which Willie had bought when on leave no doubt helped him to look smart at job interviews.

That the extra time in the Army after the war ended was interesting, useful and pleasant emerges clearly from the letters.

There was plenty of free time and no restrictions on where to go when off duty. He had a higher rank with better pay and an interesting job which earned him a glowing testimonial. All of this must have increased his chances in the job market:

I have been working hard this morning but this afternoon, by the grace of the officer, the motor cycle has been again at my disposal and a pleasant off duty trip to Valenciennes has been the result. This town is still gay with bunting which was hung out to welcome the British troops when it was recaptured. Although the town is a little damaged, particularly the railway track, which is the contour of a switchback, everything is quite gay.

Phillips accompanied me in the sidecar and we hunted around the railway canteens for tinned fruit, which is very delectable these warm spring days and cheap withal. We managed to get large tins of apricots for 1 franc 80 centimes a tin.

You know, taking one thing with another I am having a b— good time just at present. Not much work, good food, enjoyable outings and a comfortable amount of spending money. Despite all these advantages I look forward impatiently to the day when I can bid France 'good-byee'. [8/4/19]

The last letter, the 270th, not counting field postcards, is brief and quoted in full:

I AM WRITING BIG BECAUSE I'VE GOT BIG NEWS Bradley, Babb, Phillips and myself are to leave here tomorrow for concentration camp Arras. Thence on the 27th to a base post where we shall stay to be deloused, medically examined etc. before proceeding to our respective dispersal stations in England. Mine is at Oswestry. I should be home about August 4th.

Best love

Your sincere son

Willie. [19/7/19]

William Whittaker, now a civilian, returned to live with his parents at the George and Dragon hotel in Tarvin.

He quickly got a good lifetime job with Martins Bank after a successful interview at their head office in Water Street, Liverpool. He was posted to the Chester branch, just a few miles from Tarvin. A free man and not, after all, dependent on his parents.

Epilogue

William Whittaker was demobilised in August 1919 and was something of a displaced person. His whole life, before he enlisted, apart from occasional visits to the seaside, had been spent in and around his home town of Burnley. His parents had, however, moved from their home at 51 Barden Lane, Burnley, when his father gave up his job as a tobacconist in Colne Road to take up the landlordship of the George and Dragon public house in Tarvin.

Not only had Willie to make a new home in an alien environment but he did not even have a job. He was an enterprising young man however and, putting his disappointments behind him, he quickly found a good career job in the Bank of Martins and Liverpool, later Martins Bank. He was posted to Chester branch, just 5 miles from Tarvin, where he passed the Associate of the Institute of Bankers exams and was then posted to the nearby branch in Birkenhead.

When at the Chester branch he was initiated by his new colleagues playing a practical joke which was tried out on all new junior employees. He was ordered to phone a local number and ask for Mr Lyon. He did so and was informed by a long-suffering voice that this was Chester zoo!

The bank was divided for administrative purposes into districts and after a few years Willie applied to move to the Burnley district which was to have a crucial bearing on his future. He was moved to the branch in the centre of Burnley and took up residence as a paying guest at the Bay Horse hotel in Worsthorne, a nearby village. The hotel dominated the ancient square of the village and its landlord was Wilfred Latham, who was married to a first cousin of Willie's, Edna Heap, the daughter of his uncle James.

He was able to revive his old friendships, notably with his musical partner Harry Preston, now musical director of the Victoria theatre, and his old form mate at Burnley Grammar school, John Kippax, whom he had last met in Boulogne after the Armistice and with whom he enjoyed a bachelor holiday in Paris. John, with a promising career as an architect frustrated by the war, had gone into the family business as a food retailer.

Burnley was a cotton town and Worsthorne, though a charming rural village, had its own weaving mill, Gorpel. This factory was owned by a local family and one of the part owners and general manager was John Crabtree, who lived with his family on the corner of the village square diagonally opposite the Bay Horse hotel. There were four Crabtree children, two sons, Harry and Jim, and two daughters, Nellie and Margaret.

Willie and John Kippax joined the local tennis club, where they met the two girls and before long two partnerships had been formed, Nellie and Billy (as she was always to know him) and Margaret and John. Both were to lead to lifelong marriages.

Billy and Nellie had three children, Betty, who died in infancy, John and Geoffrey, who survived them. It was John who found the war letters after Nellie died and passed them on to the writer, his younger brother, much later.

Billy was soon promoted to be second man at the Bingley branch of Martins and a few years later, in 1940, to be manager of the branch in another textile town, Barnoldswick, just 12 miles from Burnley and in the Craven district of the bank.

The Second World War was at crisis point when he made what was to be his last move and Billy immediately joined the newly formed Home Guard unit. This was part of the West Riding 33rd division of the Duke of Wellington's regiment and covered Barnoldswick, the neighbouring town of Earby and the surrounding district. He was at first orderly room sergeant, exactly the job he had in the Army at the end of the First World War, but within weeks he was commissioned in the rank of Captain and made second in command.

Nellie Whittaker had barely sewn the three pips of his rank on to the epaulettes of his uniform when the commanding officer, Major Aloysius Humphries, headmaster of the local Roman Catholic primary school, died suddenly in his early forties and Billy was promoted to Major in his place, now in charge of the whole unit. The three pips were hastily unpicked and a major's crown was substituted.

Thus, William Whittaker's civilian and military duties matched exactly those of the fictitious Captain Mainwaring, hero of the ever-popular television comedy series *Dad's Army*, as officer commanding the Home Guard and the local bank manager. By coincidence, the scriptwriters of *Dad's Army* chose to call Captain Mainwaring's bank 'Swallows', clearly a take on Martins, the martin being another member of the swallow family.

The television series relies for its situation comedy on the affection in which the Home Guard was held and the many, not unkind, jokes about it. The force had only just been renamed when Billy joined, having originally been the LDV which stood for Local Defence Volunteers. This was sometimes known, rather unfairly, as the 'Look, Duck and Vanish' but more often referred to as the 'Lads, Dads and Veterans'. It was widely thought to be armed only with broom handles!

It is true that young 'lads' of seventeen or eighteen years of age were expected to join the Home Guard prior to being conscripted into the three full-time armed services. At the other end of the scale were the 'veterans', many of them 'dads', but they were not old has-beens. They were in fact seasoned men in the prime of their lives who had served in the First World War. Some of these men were ready-made NCOs, ideal instructors for the youngsters and all of them formed the backbone of what were formidable fighting units.

In line with the Dad's Army image, the forward observation posts, locations on the edges of the twin towns, were all public houses and no doubt these called for regular inspection. It was equally likely that those inspecting quenched their thirsts on arrival but these posts were in fact ideally situated if there had been an enemy invasion.

The broomsticks, if they had ever existed, were quickly replaced with rifles and the 33rd division was positively bristling with weapons including, as well as rifles, machine guns, hand grenades and sticky bombs (a fearsome anti-tank weapon, which was literally stuck on to enemy vehicles to punch holes in the armour or blow them up). If the Germans had invaded they would have had a difficult time with every town in the land defended by well-armed units, mostly made up of experienced men with detailed knowledge of the local topography.

After the war Bill Whittaker, as he was always known after his move to Barnoldswick, had a full and active life serving the local community in a variety of ways. He was treasurer of the Boy Scouts Association and chairman of the National Savings Committee. He also organised concerts in the town involving famous names such as the operatic tenor Heddle Nash and the hugely popular all-girl accordion band of Ivy Benson.

His great hobby, the violin, was not neglected. He became leader of the Colne Symphony Orchestra, a post he held for thirty years. He played in the scratch pit orchestra for the light operatic and musical comedy shows of the local choral society and at church fairs. He also played some of his First World War favourites with his wife Nellie, who was an accomplished pianist.

He retired from the bank at the age of sixty-two and lived for a further twenty-four years. He walked several miles daily and took great interest in his three grandchildren, William, Edward and Katherine, children of the writer, his son Geoffrey, and his daughter-in-law Florence. He was proud to be a highly respected figure in the town.

William Whittaker died peacefully in hospital following a stroke in 1983.

Also available from Amberley Publishing

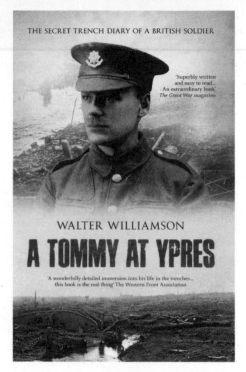

The secret trench diary of a British soldier

'A wonderfully detailed immersion into his life in the trenches ... this book is the real thing.
A lovely man; a great read' THE WESTERN FRONT ASSOCIATION

'There was a blinding flash and an ear-splitting report and the "prisoner" fell across me. The bullet had caught him full in the chin and passed out at the base of his skull.'
Within these pages lies the reality of life for a Tommy: the bravery, the warm comradeship, the gentle humour, the strength of character and resilience, the sadness, the tragedy – *A Tommy at Ypres* reveals the true spirit of an outstanding generation.

£12.99 Paperback
25 illustrations
352 pages
978-1-4456-1368-0

Available from all good bookshops or to order direct
Please call **01453-847-800**
www.amberleybooks.com